Think

like a

Tree

The
natural principles
guide to life

Sarah Spencer

ISBN 978-1-9160144-0-4

Contents

Foreword

Think about the National Forest and you'll probably visualise trees, a growing army of young saplings marching across the landscape. But of course the trees are really an expression of a bigger story; that the natural world can be a catalyst for positive and lasting change.

In the late 1980s the landscape, here in this central region of the UK, had reached a crisis point. It needed a radical re-think that would spark an upward spiral in its fortunes. That big idea was the National Forest. In less than 30 years it has spawned a remarkable healing process, restoring the environment, regenerating industry and revitalising communities.

On the face of it, this book describes the bravery of one woman to confront her own crisis point. But just as the National Forest is about so much more than trees, this book offers far more than Sarah Spencer's own story. In fact, it takes on something unexpected and ambitious; to draw on the fascinating complexities of our trees and forests, and distil a set of natural principles as a manual for the modern world.

There's no denying we need it now. Stress, obesity, asthma– barely a week goes by without another headline charting the rise of man-made problems, and that's before we throw in the damage we are doing to our environment. As humans we are all amazing and flawed in equal measure, and if we are to save ourselves from the growing threats to mental health and physical illness, we need the natural world and each other more than we care to admit.

The essential wisdom of *Think like a Tree* helps us to make these connections, showing how, in our busy lives, we can be inspired by nature to find perspective, to rebalance and ultimately to flourish. Just as in the National Forest we have set out to make woodlands a part of everyday life, so this book aims to show how a daily dose of trees can help people to develop as individuals. After all, it is our essential differences that make us who we are.

The long-term resilience of a forest is built on such diversity – each species having its own niche, the collaborative relationships, providing adaptability in the face of change. Reading Sarah's words leaves me with this over-riding essential truth; that whilst trees planted individually might struggle, those in a forest are strengthened by each other, literally drawing themselves up together towards the light.

Now surely that's a fitting message for our times.

John Everitt
Chief Executive, National Forest Company
Derbyshire UK
April 2019

About this book

This is my first book and it has been fun yet challenging to write. Thankfully I have a super-talented editor in Gina Walker, who has pored over the drafts and brought me back into line when I've strayed too far from the key concepts.

The book is a practical one and my style is quite direct – it might not suit everyone. Gina and I have had many discussions about how far to push this, for fear of putting some people off. Since there is much of my own experience and core values in this work we've gone with a relatively direct approach, which is my personal style in life.

I am someone who likes to get stuff done; I have discovered and have lived many of the ideas that are in the book, have made changes to my life (not necessarily always of my own choosing), and I know that meeting challenges head-on has worked for me. I am someone who believes that life should be an effort and that effort brings happiness (as you'll find in a later chapter), which I realise runs counter to the direction we are often pulled in the modern world, where we are told we should do everything to make our lives easier. Taking the more difficult road can be scary and uncomfortable but it's worth the energy, in my experience.

There are many books out there that will encourage you to do what *feels* right – this book is more about doing what *is* right – right for you, right for other people, and right for the rest of the living world. Of course this book is only my interpretation of what *is* right, but I hope there will be enough ideas for you to continue your own journey.

Furthermore, an active approach seems right at the current time, when there is certainly much to be done. We have challenging tasks ahead. People around the world are struggling, due to physical and psychological ill-health; other living beings (plants, animals etc) are dying at unprecedented rates and, as I write, the UN states that we have 12 years to take action on our warming world.[1] I believe we can all play our part, but only if we are up for the challenge.

In writing this book I acknowledge that I am not an expert, but I don't see that as a disadvantage. I have tried to bring in research, theories and ideas from a wide range of disciplines: from biology, psychology, ecology, education, therapies, and many other fields, and have sought to take a big-picture approach to bringing ideas into my work. My own life experience has also given me some interesting insights, and perhaps a different perspective on life, which I hope you will find helpful.

None of the suggestions I give in the book should be interpreted as medical advice, and I recommend that you consult a medical professional where appropriate. My day-to-day work does not involve giving advice on health, either physical or psychological, and simply gives a framework for people to find their own way forward, guided by principles inspired by trees and the rest of the living world.

I hope that you find the exercises helpful too – they have been trialled by myself and course participants. But of course, they only work if you do them! Above all, please enjoy the journey and share your learning, experience and encouragement with others.

Preface – How I got here

I use the natural principles described in this book to guide me every day. But I didn't always (well not consciously anyway).

I grew up in Charnwood Forest in the centre of England, and my childhood was spent making dens and climbing trees. As I became a teenager, life wasn't so great. Walks and horse rides in the woods became my escape from life, bullying and depression. By the age of 16 I was regularly visiting the doctor with many diverse physical illnesses, that I later found out were causing my mental health problems and were not a result of them, as was frequently suggested. Determined not to let my health rule my life, I went to university, got married, developed a career as a legal representative to refugees, and had three wonderful children. We bought a smallholding in the National Forest[1] in Derbyshire in 2003 and I immersed myself in my love of gardening, growing, trees and woods. I trained as a forest school practitioner,[2] inspired by the desire to get children into the outdoors. We developed our house and land using principles from permaculture[3] and I completed a course in ecological design[4] with ten diverse designs from our smallholding, a local school garden, and my biggest project – a community woodland social enterprise called Whistlewood Common.[5]

Whistlewood is a 10-acre field owned by a pioneering 400 (and counting) people who bought shares in 2013, and over the next five years transformed it into a thriving community woodland. We planted 3500 trees, including 150 fruit and nut trees, built a straw bale roundhouse, and run workshops and community events designed to support anyone who wants to make positive choices about the way they live.

But the illness raised its head again and I spent most of 2015 into 2016 in bed, going to numerous hospital appointments in a wheelchair after collapses and seizures on top of my growing list of symptoms. I was misdiagnosed as having a stroke, and lost the ability to remember, read or stand upright. My most fundamental functions such as heart rate, breathing, temperature regulation and balance went haywire and I had brain fog so bad I couldn't think straight. My muscles ached and felt like I was wading through treacle. I had a constant electrical feeling in my body and brain as if I had been plugged into the mains. It was the neurological symptoms that were the most distressing – my personality changed, I became angry, tearful, paranoid and incredibly hard to live with. And my mood changed from one minute to the next. The slightest trigger, from food and smells to stress, would set me off. My husband and kids are saints for putting up with me, and it put an incredible amount of strain on everyone.

The low point was my birthday in April 2016, which I will never forget. My family went to a local restaurant for lunch, but I was so weak that I had to be taken in a wheelchair. I resolved at the end of the meal that things would change, that I would seek a diagnosis, and change whatever I had to in order to become well again.

Over the course of the next year I used my natural design skills to plan a roadmap to pull me back to health. I researched potential illnesses and treatments, sought out new medical practitioners, and eventually received two diagnoses that finally made sense and accounted for all of my symptoms. The approach of seeing myself as a whole person rather than a set of unrelated symptoms (as the medical profession did) paid off. It was my immune system that was going haywire, and it appeared there was a genetic link but the principal cause was the environmental factors that I had known for so long were triggers. So I changed my diet, and now avoid smells, chemicals, toiletries, washing powders, stress (as much as I can!) and a host of other things. And I set about retraining my brain to stop working against me and start working for me. I try to make the most of what I can do rather than focusing on what I can't do. When your energy is in short supply, it doesn't pay to waste it worrying about (or doing) pointless things. My diet is radical (I discovered that the healthy fruit and vegetables that I was growing were making me ill), and I am intolerant to most complementary therapies, supplements and conventional medicines. I am also exercise intolerant. To be honest, I have a regime that most fussy toddlers or teenagers would find attractive (except without the sweets). But the main thing that I realised through all of this was that I was unique. When I am asked what I did to recover, I don't share my routine – I tell the person asking that they have to find their own way, because they are unique too. I wouldn't get far selling the book entitled *The 20 Safe Foods, No-Vegetables, No-Exercise Programme* – or maybe I would, but for all the wrong reasons! Instead, the courses that I have developed now support people in finding ways that are unique to them, guided by natural principles and a design cycle that allows them to put those principles into practice.

As life continued, the importance of the things that make nature work – like valuing uniqueness, feedback, self-regulation, efficient energy use and avoiding pointless battles (often with myself) – became even more apparent.

Once I was sufficiently recovered, I had to decide what I was going to do next with my life. I could no longer do physical work – gardening, designing outdoor spaces, or working with children – as I used to. But my passion was still with the outdoors, and now, increasingly, with nature connection and wellbeing. So I designed a livelihood that could balance my health, my passions, and what I see as my purpose in life. That meant turning to teaching short courses, creating online courses, and of course this book, which I'm writing while looking out of my window on the days that I have less energy.

I now live every day by the natural principles that I discovered during this process, and I will share how I use them throughout the book. All of this has made me happier than I have ever been. Having a chronic illness is not fun – it's hard work, frustrating, and emotionally and physically draining. It has an impact on everyone around me, which is the part I hate the most. But it has taught me what is fundamentally important in life. The clarity that was revealed is uplifting and empowering, comforting and fulfilling. I feel part of something bigger and more connected than just me and my problems, and that makes me happy to be alive.

Think like a Tree

Part 1

Woodland wisdom

Thinking like a tree

You've probably picked up this book with a certain curiosity about the title. Maybe your first response is *"but trees don't think"*, or perhaps you are curious about whether trees have intelligence and what form that intelligence might take. First I need to make it clear – trees don't think (sorry to burst your bubble). They don't have a brain and they are very different from humans in that regard. But they are aware, and can sense their surroundings in a variety of different ways. They can remember, and can even pass memories between generations.[1] They may even have a sort of 'heartbeat' – (they have been shown to contract and expand as they pump water through their systems).[2] Amazingly, we know that plants even have an imagination – to be able to react to something that isn't actually there.[3] This last talent has been demonstrated in the humble pea, and it seems likely that trees react in the same way. These many abilities have been demonstrated in research, but plant biologists are only just out of the starting blocks in terms of what there is still to learn. Watching the science unfold is exciting, and new discoveries are turning on their head many of the myths traditionally surrounding seemingly passive plants. Many more examples of the amazing lives of trees (and other plants) will be revealed throughout the book, with references to the relevant research.

While we know that trees lack consciousness, they possess the ability to know what they are supposed to be doing, and how to do it in the most effective way possible. In that regard I believe trees may have the upper hand over humans. They may not be able to write the *Complete Works of Shakespeare*, or create a beautiful symphony, but they are highly effective, adaptable, resilient and can pass on what they've learned to future generations. And they don't come with the downsides of human behaviour – the capacity for self-destruction that we have on individual, societal and planetary levels.

So if trees can't think, what is this all about? Well this book asks you to do the thinking – so brace yourself for the challenge of seeing trees, and yourself, in a different light. I would like to explore with you the wisdom that trees can share with us about living a better life.

Common ancestors

Several hundred million generations ago, you and the tree in your local park shared a common ancestor. Of course that ancestor did not look like a woody plant with a trunk, nor like an ape as you are; but they were made of carbon, and cells and chromosomes, just like us. Our modern versions share some of the same DNA, although many trees have more DNA than us. One species of birch, for example, has 112 chromosomes to our 46. Surprisingly, some of the genes implicated in human diseases have been found in plants. The genome of *Arabidopsis thaliana* (a plant in the brassica family) contains the *BRCA* breast cancer gene, for example.

Animals split from plants early in the history of life – around 1.5 billion years ago – and since then plants and animals (and later humans) have taken very different evolutionary paths. Over hundreds of millions of generations, we have moved further and further from knowing that we are all related. When Charles Darwin published *On The Origin Of Species* in 1859,[4] this knowledge began to be brought into scientific certainty, and the biochemical basis of our evolutionary relatedness was revealed by the discovery of the double helix structure of DNA in the 1950s.

By that time, we were very much rooted in the idea that humans are separate from the natural world. This was compounded by religious and philosophical teachings going back millennia, which promoted the world view that humans are at the top of the pile, with all other living things relegated to inferior bit-parts, and valued only by their usefulness to people. Of course that view still persists today. Humans are in fact just one of the branches on the tree of life and it could be argued that that we evolved into *Homo sapiens* so recently that we have not yet had time to prove our long-term resilience.

Even the language we use to describe the natural world is loaded with cultural and historical meaning. Anthropomorphism (attributing human characteristics to non-human entities, such as animals or plants) is widespread, and may be considered as one factor in our problematic relationship with the natural world by assigning higher value to beings that share human characteristics. When describing the natural world it is difficult to avoid some human-centred vocabulary creeping in. I realise, now that I'm writing, that we have much better language for describing humans than for describing the living world, and the temptation to fill the vast gaps in our knowledge with our own views and feelings is inevitable. Many writers on the natural world, including Darwin, struggled with this. *"I have often personified the word Nature for I have found it difficult to avoid this ambiguity."*

During these millennia we also lost sight of the fact that everything that sustains us originates as a plant. Plants convert the Sun's energy into nutrients, and we eat those nutrients, or we eat animals or fungi that consume plants. It's also interesting to consider that animals (including humans) developed the ability to move (seen as one of our superior characteristics as compared to trees), due to a fundamental design flaw – we can't synthesise our own food. The seemingly passive oak tree down your street, that you ignore every day on the way to work, can stand still and turn carbon dioxide from the air into matter – trunks, branches and leaves. You can't do the same to make arms and legs and fingers, so you have to go and look for your food in your lunch hour – food that originated with plants.

All this leads me to believe that it's not a bad idea to get to know the hand (the leaf) that feeds us in a bit more detail.

Problem solving

We share with all plants problem-solving abilities that deal with surprisingly similar fundamental issues. Until relatively recently, humans and plants shared the same environments, subject to the same pressures and external influences. Despite many of us now living in centrally heated homes, with TVs and the internet, we still have the same very basic needs, such as food, water, security and connection. However, humans have the addition of a brain, which complicates things and often takes us away from these core requirements. While trees evolved around 280 million years ago, modern humans have been around just a few hundred thousand years, so it seems likely we could learn a thing or two from them.

Janine Benyus[5] is an innovation consultant and author of books on biomimicry,[6] which aims to solve complex human problems using inspiration from models, systems and elements in nature. She believes that we should be apprentices of all living things, learning all we can from them to improve every aspect of our lives. As humans, when we want to solve problems we turn to experts – teachers, scientists, craftspeople and engineers – but we have been ignoring the artists, builders, artisans, engineers, biologists and chemists that are living all around us in the natural world. They can build materials stronger than steel and tougher than ceramics, and do this without heat or toxic chemicals. They can withstand pressure, heat, drought, drying out, flooding and more. Trees can create colour without pigment – for example, the blue quandong tree in Australia creates cobalt blue using a submicroscopic surface structure that reflects blue light. To do this, it must be constructed with a precision of a few millionths of a millimetre. Some human scientists, farmers and product engineers already learn from, and copy, plants. Take Velcro, inspired by burrs that stick to animal fur; or more recently, desalination processes based on the ingenious ways in which mangroves remove salt from sea water. Take a look at www.AskNature.org[7] to see how nature solves design and engineering problems that biomimetic designers are now emulating.

Permaculture, an earlier nature-inspired design system, originated in the 1970s when its founders Bill Mollison and David Holmgren observed that the same principles that apply to nature could be used to design sustainable and productive agricultural systems.[8] There are now permaculture associations, projects, farms and communities around the world, following a set of ethics and principles that address many of the agricultural problems that have led to high chemical fertiliser and pesticide use, plant resistance, erosion and destruction of native forests for agriculture. In addition, regenerative agriculture, agroforestry and holistic grazing are food production systems that regenerate land, build healthy soil, and lock in carbon, while producing abundant food. These systems pave the way to produce healthy food for billions of people, with many fewer harmful impacts on natural ecosystems.

The Transition movement,[9] regenerative culture, systems-based management practices and economic models that take into account environmental and social factors all take the learning into the social and economic spheres, stressing that we cannot have unlimited growth on a finite planet.

These disciplines look at the practical agricultural, engineering and economic benefits of learning from nature, but practitioners have now logically expanded into exploring the social and personal benefits of learning from the natural world. Ecopsychologists, permaculture practitioners, holistic thinkers, biomimetic designers and natural therapists are leading the way.

This is where *Think like a Tree* enters the party, following in the footsteps of pioneers and established practitioners, and learning from the significant and expanding body of research that examines the concept of nature-inspired problem solving.

But of course learning from nature has been around for millennia. Early humans absorbed knowledge by being perpetually immersed in nature, and adapting it for their own use – for example, when they took the idea of sitting under the shade of a tree, and used it to fabricate their own sunshades. We are born mimics, copying each other's behaviour. So it is only logical that people connected with their ecosystems would emulate the behaviour of those around them, human or non-human – whether it be copying a pack of wolves as they corner their prey, or mimicking the ways beavers modify rivers.

Leonardo da Vinci stated *"If you do not rest on the good foundations of nature you will labour with little honour and less profit"*. He studied and recorded the behaviour of birds extensively before designing his flying machines. Charles Darwin and subsequent plant biologists and geneticists opened our eyes to the wonderful problem-solving abilities of plants. And more recently Sir David Attenborough shared his wisdom that *"There are some four million different kinds of animals and plants in the world. Four million different solutions to the problems of staying alive"*.

Today many indigenous peoples around the world have deeply intimate relationships with the environments that sustain every aspect of their lives.

The trouble with brains

We've established that trees and humans share fundamental common ground, but we can't ignore the fact that we are very different. Our brain is unique and adds a vast layer of complexity. People have the ability to decide what to do, but we can also decide not to do things. When an anorexic teenager doesn't eat, a desperate person self-harms, an addict damages their body, or a business-person stays up all night for a deadline, they 'choose' (sometimes in the loosest sense of the word) not to follow a basic instinct. Conscious thought is a wonderful thing that gives us all sorts of advantages and benefits. However, it also allows us to go against the fundamental drivers that we all have within us, but that trees can't fail to follow. Humans have to think about doing the right thing, rather than just doing it.

Until 70 thousand years ago, humans lived in very similar ways to other animals, but around that time a cognitive revolution began. We developed the ability to think about, and communicate, ideas that weren't based in the concrete realities of daily life – i.e. theories, beliefs and myths. This made us fundamentally different from the rest of the living world. We could now accelerate human evolution, facilitated by the more advanced ways of communicating and the ability to transfer adaptive advantages by packets of learned information, rather than purely by genetics (DNA). This incredible evolution has makes us the most complex single organism on the planet. However, added complexity leads to added problems, such as self-destructive behaviours, and these can even take us away from the most basic needs, such as the desire to survive, to live, to belong, and to grow. Our brains give us the option to procrastinate, to knowingly make ourselves ill, to consciously hurt others, to go to war, to destroy our own surroundings, and lead some people to make a conscious decision to end their own life.

With regard to our relationship with other people and other species, humans have developed to the extent that we are divorced from the surroundings that we rely on for life (for example, plants for food, clean air, clean water). Around 12,000 years ago the agricultural revolution began, and people gradually settled down to have control over the plants and herds of animals around them. Somewhat surprisingly, this led to humans having a more limited and unhealthier diet (mostly grain-based), they worked harder, had more children (and more mouths to feed), they destroyed more forests to set aside for agriculture, had more wars, and created an elite that forced them to work harder for less food. People took on the backbreaking jobs that plants had been doing for them for free, such as irrigation, pest control, soil stabilisation, adding fertility to the earth and feeding animals. From then on, there was no going back and, now that we are people living in the twenty-first century, neither would we want to. However, we now find ourselves in a situation where we have very little direct relationship to the natural world, and because we don't immediately feel the consequences of our actions, we have few of the natural feedback mechanisms that would bring our behaviour back to a healthy equilibrium for us and for the other living things with whom we share our planet. We are currently living in the 'anthropocene'[10] era, characterised by humans' overwhelming impact on the entire planet, and we are the cause of only the sixth mass extinction the world has ever seen. Of course, this is not a modern phenomenon – humans have been hunting animals and destroying plants to extinction for tens of thousands of years. *Homo sapiens* was also responsible for the demise of the other *Homo* species. However, in modern times our impact has accelerated to the extent that, according to a 2018 report by the World Wildlife Fund (WWF), wildlife populations have plummeted by 60% in less than 50 years.[11] A broken industrial growth system has fuelled a society that is trashing planetary resources at an unprecedented rate.

But what worries me is not simply the loss of wondrous plant and animal life, but the harm it is doing to us as people. I consider myself unlucky and lucky in equal measure. I live with an immune-related illness that was triggered by – and is made worse by – contact with any number of stimuli encountered in the modern world. This has given me insight into the harm that we, as individuals and as a society, are doing to ourselves. Non-communicable diseases, such as cardiovascular disease, cancer, auto-immune disease, dementia, diabetes, allergies and obesity-related illness, are on the rise.[12] In developed countries these illnesses have become more prevalent during the last 100 years, but developing countries are now seeing the same transition from communicable and infectious diseases, to non-communicable disease.

Our brains are being subjected to similar levels of ill-health, with resulting mental disorders such as anxiety, depression, neuropsychiatric disease, self-harm, substance abuse and suicide. A recent study estimated that 1.1 billion people around the world had a mental or substance-misuse disorder in 2016, with the rates in developed countries estimated, on average, higher than elsewhere. In the UK in 2016 around 18% of the population were estimated to have a mental disorder, and in the USA 21.5%.[13]

Our conscious brains are in overdrive, trying to cope with too many competing choices and stimuli. I have always had a brain without an off-switch, something I considered a benefit when in education, but which came back to bite me when it contributed to my health problems. Our unconscious minds are overworked too. Short-term stress responses (fight, flight or freeze) are essential if you encounter an angry bear, but the constant stresses of modern life cause hormones like cortisol and adrenaline to be pumped into the bloodstream, without the release valves, such as exercise and rest, that allow them to be brought back down to baseline levels. In the 2016 study mentioned above, 6% of people in the USA were estimated to be suffering specifically from anxiety disorders, with a rate of 5% in the UK.

Children and young people are particularly affected. In the UK, anxiety disorders are highest in the 15–19 age group (an estimated 6.35% of 15–19-year-olds in 2016), with children aged 10–14 only marginally behind at 5.83%. In the USA, the figures are 6.51% for 15–19 years, and 4.65% for 10–14 years.[14]

A 2017 UK study conducted by NHS Digital stated that a whopping 12.8% of 5–19-year-olds met the criteria for at least one mental disorder.[15]

To be a successful human in the twenty-first century it is no longer an option to simply follow basic instincts. Instead we must actively use our minds to make positive decisions that come naturally elsewhere in nature. This involves effort, engagement and developing a conscious way of living.

> *"Modern man talks of the battle with nature, forgetting that if he ever won the battle he would find himself on the losing side."*
>
> E.F. Schumacher

Living consciously

You will probably see the irony in looking at trees, which are unconscious, in order to learn how to live more consciously – to choose to live in a way that is healthy and that regenerates our lives and our surroundings for us and future generations. But we can improve our minds by dialling back the levels of complexity in our lives. We can reconnect with the basic needs of comfort, security, self-esteem, belonging, human interaction and a relationship with the natural world, in order to make our lives more fulfilled. Once we have developed firm roots, it becomes much easier to build the top growth.

But to do this you must decide to be in the driving seat, take an active part, and get your head in the game. Alternatively, you can decide to do nothing and be a passenger, a victim, or be used or exploited by someone else. The sad fact is if you don't make a decision to design your life then someone else will do it for you. There is no neutral approach. That person might be someone you know, like a partner, family member or boss; or it might be an advertising executive, company CEO or media mogul. Unless we delve more deeply, the choices that we think we have, like choosing a shampoo or a variety of apple, become smokescreens, obscuring the things that could fundamentally make a difference, like the pursuit of fulfilment and belonging. Having many different, insignificant choices is paralysing, not empowering. Encouraging people to always want more is also a very good tactic for keeping them quiet. There is nothing so problematic for marketers than people saying *"I'm OK thanks without that extra consumer item"*.

Modern human definitions of success include income, financial wealth, material goods, fame and out-competing others – which leads to damaging consumption, wasteful use of resources and increasing inequality. In my workshops I ask participants how they think nature defines success and they come up with words like growth, co-operation, harmony, supportive

9

relationships, resilience, vitality, new life, regeneration, lack of waste, and diversity. Every group comes up with very similar suggestions – I'm sure the same ideas would come out of workshops all over the world. I then ask who wants to live like that – and everyone says "yes please!".

Don't be put off by the critics who say that if we try and change our broken system we would all be back living in caves and wearing hair shirts – that's just an excuse for inaction and to keep people consuming. This is about creating something better for us, together, for which there are already solutions. It's time for us to write our own stories, with the natural world as our guide. Every tree that has ever lived has changed the planet and left it a better place than when it started out. It has pulled carbon dioxide from thin air to create soil; it has given out life-sustaining oxygen, regulating the atmosphere; it has contributed to creating rain; and it has hosted other species that have produced a wondrous diversity of life on a planet that was once bare rock and gas. It hasn't done that without effort, and neither will you, but if you think you can't change the world then remember those trees and think again.

The benefits of being in nature

When I was little I kept falling in ponds. Not just one pond but six in one year! None of my tumbles were life-threatening but my mother despaired and started to bring a change of clothes whenever we went out. I was clearly fascinated with what was in the water, and was later grateful that my nature-loving mum wasn't a risk-averse parent who might have sat me in front of a screen instead, for fear of me drowning. Now that I am an adult, and my balance is a little better, I still love ponds. I've created two largish ones in my woodland and love to spend time sitting near them watching the pond skaters, swallows and dragonflies. I feel my blood pressure lower, my (normally erratic) heart rate slow, and I have the strong urge to breathe deeply. I feel a connection.

That connection was clearly activated at an early age, but it has kept me coming back for more over the years, and even when I lived in London in my early twenties I would regularly seek out the local park or head for the countryside. Connection gives a hit of pleasure as powerful as any drug, and without any negative side-effects. It helps to balance the dysfunctional mix of chemicals and hormones swirling around my body.

Research has subsequently proved right my early instincts about the benefits of being in nature. Here's what the UK Government's 25-year environment plan, published in 2018, has to say:

"Spending time in the natural environment – as a resident or a visitor – improves our mental health and feelings of wellbeing. It can reduce stress, fatigue, anxiety and depression. It can help boost immune systems, encourage physical activity and may reduce the risk of chronic diseases such as asthma. It can combat loneliness and bind communities together."[1]

Studies show that contact with nature lowers stress. Links are similarly made to a lower incidence of cardiovascular and respiratory tract illness, lower levels of hypertension, better recovery times, better mood, improved sleep, increased levels of wellbeing and vitality, better self-regulation, and to a positive overall effect on mental health.[2] Nature will also help you concentrate. There are even proven benefits from looking at pictures of nature while stuck indoors – for example, when recovering in hospital (although pictures are, unsurprisingly, less effective than actually being in nature).

A discipline of Ecotherapy, or Nature Therapy, has grown up, covering a wide range of beneficial activities. Green gyms provide outdoor exercise with a purpose, such as conservation or tree-planting. Even running in the outdoors has been shown to be more beneficial than the equivalent amount of exercise in the gym.[3] Horticultural therapy has similar beneficial effects, with participants feeling the positive emotions from watching the fruits of their labour grow, combined with fresh air and moderate exercise (gardening involves a lot of bending and stretching, and is good for flexibility too).

Talking therapy that takes place in the outdoors (sometimes also confusingly called Ecotherapy) is another growing discipline. In my view all therapists should try and get their clients outdoors, where the forest would do some of the work for them. Doctors could prescribe a range of outdoor activities for patients (known as 'Green Prescribing' and already taking place in some areas). Being outdoors also facilitates a shift from the traditional inward-looking focus, to looking at oneself in the wider environmental context. Depression and anxiety often lead a sufferer to turn inwards, and my (admittedly unprofessional) experience is that traditional therapy, talking and medical, can compound feelings of guilt (*"It's my fault, I'll only feel better if I can change myself"*), rather than focusing on the environment you live in (*"I'll feel better if I change where and how I spend my time "*).

Forest Bathing has been receiving lots of publicity recently. Originating in Japan, and called *Shinrin-yoku*, it involves organised groups walking and sitting in the forest, using all the senses and often undertaking guided meditation. A study of 24 *Shinrin-yoku* forest areas in Japan showed that participants had lower stress levels, blood pressure and pulse than the equivalent participation in city environments.[4]

For those who don't have much time, the good news is that you can feel some improvement in your mood after just 10 minutes of exposure (for example touching a tree, or even a piece of wood).

Connecting with nature and the *Think like a Tree* principles also sit firmly within the UK Government's *Five Ways to Mental Wellbeing*.[5] These five ways, in the context of the outdoors, are:

- **Connecting** – with the natural world and each other
- **Being active** – in the outdoors regularly and repeatedly in different ways
- **Noticing** – each other, the changing seasons, our own growth and development, the natural world
- **Learning** – about each other and the natural world, learning new skills
- **Giving** – time and attention to each other as well as giving something back to the natural spaces used, through caring, planting, managing and understanding them.

As you can see, simply being in the outdoors does not give the full picture when it comes to wellbeing – to reap the maximum benefit it is vital to go beyond that to make a connection with nature. Research from the University of Derby[6] has revealed that there are five pathways to nature connection:

- **Senses** – engaging all the senses
- **Emotions** – connecting with feelings of joy, wonder, calm and so on
- **Beauty** – appreciating landscapes or small details, and then being able to express those feelings
- **Meaning** – exploring what nature means: metaphor, symbolism and language. This is a thinking process.
- **Compassion** – extending our sense of who we are to include nature, and to care for living things.

My own view is that nature connection shouldn't involve stand-alone activities (*"I'm going outside to get my hit of nature connection today"*), but should be woven into other parts of your life, like walking to the shops or to work, gardening, or joining a conservation group. For example, a friend of mine has taken up horse logging on the weekend (timber extraction with horses is a method of maintaining forests that is less damaging than using modern machinery). Another chooses a cafe that is half an hour away to meet friends for coffee, so she has to walk through the countryside to get there. A third walks to the local shops rather than driving, and although this is through the town, there are still a number of trees and urban green spaces that she purposefully notices on the way, observing how they change with the seasons. Weaving nature connection into your routine means it becomes embedded in your life. Our ancient and our recent ancestors would have obtained their nature fix ('Vitamin N')[7] from meaningful activity.

However, it might be worth remarking that your relationship with nature will not necessarily be a pleasant one every day, just as your human relationships (however close) have good days and bad days. Being soaked by an unexpected downpour or tripping over a fallen log come with the territory, but the benefits far outweigh the occasional irritation. When it comes to weather I like to live by the saying, *"there is no such thing as bad weather, only unsuitable clothing"*.

Passing through natural environments without engaging with them won't give you the greatest benefits. Using the outdoors simply as a venue for exercise with your headphones on, or walking the dog while thinking about work is not enough. You have to engage.

However, the good news is that once you start, it feels entirely natural – because that's what we evolved to do.

Note that none of these pathways to connection involve being able to name 50 different species of plant or animal (phew, that lets me off the hook!). Neither do we need to know the uses for plants or trees, nor feel that we must have dominance over, or fear, nature. These ways of looking at the world may even have contributed to the destruction of living things that we have been witnessing for the last few centuries.

Past relationships with nature haven't worked, but there is a blueprint for a new relationship, based on connection. This nature–connection model gives us free rein to express our emotions, unleash our inner poet, and – dare I say it – free that tree hugger who has been in there waiting to get out.

And, as if that wasn't enough, increased nature connection has been shown to increase positive environmental behaviours too. So it's a win–win: for you, your descendants and the planet.[8]

So how does *Think like a Tree* relate to the benefits of being in nature and the five pathways to connection? Well, it involves all five, with a particular focus on meaning – what we can learn from living beings. It's an active thinking process – one that takes effort, and requires reflection, both inward and outward. It will potentially throw up uncomfortable emotions, but it will be worth it, I promise. Start by reconnecting with that one moment in your childhood where you fell in a pond, marvelled at a landscape or studied the bark of a tree – where did you first make that connection?

So now you know the benefits – what are you waiting for?

Exercise

Three Good Things in Nature

Every day notice three good things in nature. Write a sentence for each of the three good things. You might note the beauty of small things at any one moment, like sights, sounds or patterns. Or it might be recording feelings or wider aspects that arise from attending to the diversity and wonder of the natural world around you. For example, it could be as seemingly trivial as noticing the song of a robin or the movement of a tree in the breeze. Set yourself a reminder to record three things every day. If you use Twitter, you can use the hashtag #3naturethings

The *Three Good Things in Nature* exercise was devised by Dr Miles Richardson from the University of Derby, and has proven benefits for wellbeing.[9]

Why learn from trees?

This book could have been called *Think like an Ecosystem* or *Think like an Ocean*, but for various reasons I settled on trees. Firstly it will not surprise you that I love trees. It may surprise you that I can't name that many outside of our British natives (to my shame and thanks to my very poor memory) – but I love being in woodlands and everything they represent.

Most people, all round the globe, live within easy reach of forests, woodlands or trees. Even in our most densely populated cities there are parks and other open spaces where they thrive, and this gives opportunities for learning from these gentle giants directly. Humans have traditionally had deep cultural relationships with trees, creating books, poems and celebrations about these wise cousins of ours. From the Ents in *Lord of the Rings* or Grandmother Willow in *Pocahontas* to the Whomping Willow in the *Harry Potter* series (and many, more literary, examples), trees are loved and are a source of inspiration. Many of our towns and cities are named after trees, like Hollywood, Sevenoaks, Ashbourne, York and New York (the latter two are named after the yew).

I know of very few people who dislike trees – other than perhaps council officials determined to tidy obsessively or eliminate risk, or developers who want to cut them down to build shopping centres. But even they are likely to appreciate a tree somewhere in their environment and find joy in the bird song that emanates from it. So, with trees, there is an opportunity for connection and for direct learning, and this book encourages you to learn just as much from the single tree in the middle of a city street as from the giant forests that sweep across our world. Don't feel that you have to travel for miles to 'get out into nature' – nature is all around you; you won't have to go far to find it. When you see a buddleia pushing its way through a crack in urban tarmac, you are witnessing an example of resilience and the overwhelming urge to keep growing whatever life's struggles. That said, the same principles outlined in this book apply to other ecosystems – natural grasslands, wetlands, shorelines and oceans, so if those are in reach I encourage you to go outside and learn from them too.

You might ask why not compare animals instead? Scientists have spent decades (and centuries) studying animal behaviour and comparing it to humans, looking at intelligence and conducting experiments on creatures to ascertain their responses to pain and other stimuli. The vast majority of nature programmes on TV focus on animals. Plants have received much less attention, beyond their agricultural value. But animals, and especially mammals, are our close evolutionary cousins. If we only study human or animal behaviour, we see a fraction of the diversity life has to offer. The further back in the evolutionary tree we go, the more the fundamental similarities, common to all life, start to emerge. When we get back to the principles that all living things have in common we are really down to the bare necessities of life. Of course not every tree will exhibit these principles in the same way, just as there are people with different preferences, needs and strengths, but as you get to know the different trees and people within the book, you will see that we have more in common than you might initially think possible.

I hope that the book will encourage you to get out and learn from nature directly and that you will have a few light-bulb moments, as I have, during my exploration of these natural principles.

Part 2

Introducing the natural principles

"The big artist keeps an eye on nature and steals her tools"
Thomas Eakins

There are patterns common to all living things. These have been developed into a set of principles. I've gathered some from permaculture, some from biomimicry, and others I have simply observed myself in nature, when walking in forests, woodlands, gardens, moors, seashores, mountains and grasslands. These patterns and principles are all around us, hiding in plain sight.

Some of the principles overlap and some contain paradoxes. They are not definitive. This book is about my own interpretation of them – I make suggestions and I hope you will take from them what you need. I encourage you to discover your own interpretations and your own principles while reading the book and during your wanderings outdoors.

Something that has intrigued me, while undertaking the research for this book, is how many studies into better ways to experience life as a human being support (without realising it) the learning explicit in these principles. These include studies on psychology, neurology, longevity, communication, human behaviour, management, economics and social networks. The more we find out, the more we see how similar we are to trees and vice versa. What works for them works for us at a fundamental level. For example, longevity studies reveal that people with a supportive network of friends live much longer than those who are lonely, and we see this in trees that are alone versus trees in forests. Giant redwoods were brought to England in Victorian times but each tree has grown only a fraction of the height of its American cousins – the principal reason being that in California they live in forests that support and nurture them. Their fellow trees provide shade, protection, ideal soil conditions, and many other benefits. Our own support networks provide us with similar advantages. More comparisons with research can be found throughout the book.

18

Many of the principles can also be found in old proverbs and ancient wisdom – for example, *"slow and steady wins the race"*, *"make hay when the sun shines"*, *"your efforts will bear fruit"*. These principles are not mere analogies, they are evolutionary success stories, tried and tested over hundreds of millions of years.

Each principle applies to living matter, but can also apply to thought patterns and human activities. For example, the principle *Slow and small solutions* applies to:

- the slow growth of trees and woods
- growth of all living tissue (each cell division creating two new cells on the same blueprint as the original, using recognised building blocks)
- planning for success (like aiming to integrate healthy eating into your daily life rather than attempting a crash diet)
- thought patterns (slow and small solutions are less likely to result in frustration, feelings of failure and burn-out).

By mimicking life's patterns we can fast-track success, avoid failure and build resilience.

Six groups of principles have emerged

Group 1   **Observation** – principles about looking, learning and being

Group 2   **Purpose** – principles about doing and growing

Group 3   **Surroundings** – principles about needs, wellbeing, health and place

Group 4   **Connection** – principles about belonging, connecting, communicating and sharing

Group 5   **Resilience** – principles about surviving, healing, adapting and rejuvenation

Group 6   **Future** – principles about regeneration, creating and celebrating

You will also find additional principles highlighted in bold throughout the book.

How to use the principles

The principles can be used in many different ways – for example, as:

- a guide to living a happy, healthy and fulfilled life
- an everyday reference to keep you on track
- a roadmap for going where you want to go
- a source of tools to help solve problems
- a way to make choices and decisions
- uplifting inspiration to know that you are not alone in life's ups and downs
- a way of seeing yourself in the context of the wonder of life on our unique planet.

Many people have already used this wisdom. *Anne Frank's Diary* has an entry about the horse chestnut tree that she could see from the window of the attic where she was in hiding. She wrote that she was inspired with hope when she saw its bare branches and knew that they would burst into life in spring. Writers, poets, artists, indigenous peoples and nature-lovers have been observing nature's principles for hundreds or thousands of years – it's time to open up their beauty and power to everyone.

Case studies

There are millions of ordinary people already learning from nature, so I set out to find just some of them. They are applying their learning in many different areas of life:

- mental health
- psychological wellbeing
- physical health
- overcoming a life challenge
- relationship issues
- employment
- leisure

- business management
- community, and more.

Basically, the natural principles apply to everything! People have been generous in sharing their stories and I have woven some of these into the book as case studies, in addition to my own experiences.

Think like a Tree

Part 3

The natural principles

Group 1 Principles

Observation

Observe and interact

"There are always flowers for those that want to see them"
Henri Matisse

People often look at me as if I'm bonkers when I say that trees can see. But when you think about it, it's obvious that trees and plants can 'see' because we can observe them angling their leaves towards the light and moving to track the Sun through the day. This is easier to notice with sunflowers, but time-lapse photography of trees shows they do the same.

Trees and plants also use light to know when to flower. Gardeners often take advantage of this. At the Chelsea Flower Show in London each May, exhibitors trick plants into flowering out of season by subjecting them to artificial dark and light regimes, and then bring them out ready for a final flourish. Amazingly, plants and humans share the same genes for sensing night and day – yet more proof that we are related in more ways than you might think.

Plants can even differentiate between colours (blue is the colour that they prefer bending towards) and, unlike us, they can detect ultraviolet and infrared light. They can 'smell' too – ethylene causes apples to ripen in sequence after one fruit detects a waft from another. They can recognise the saliva of insects and can remember things such as day length. To learn more about how trees perceive what's around them I recommend the book *What A Plant Knows* by biologist Daniel Chamovitz,[1] a fascinating analysis of the full range of plant senses, along with the relevant scientific research.

Our human senses may not be exactly the same, but this group of principles is all about how we can employ them to our full advantage, just like trees do. When we learn how to harness the powers of observation, everything else follows, and we can take in information from our surroundings, and process it to best benefit us.

Despite having a wide range of ways to perceive the world, we don't use them all of the time. Our senses 'turn off and on', depending on our circumstances. Our brains would be subjected to information overload without some means of filtering our sensory input. I have personal experience of sensory overload during migraine attacks, when every sense is heightened (lights, sounds, touch, smell) to the point of being unbearable. Even in normal circumstances we 'turn off' our senses to be able to cope with the mass of sights and sounds in the modern world, but we often forget to turn them back on again. We wander through life like zombies, blocking out the good information along with the bad. When was the last time you heard bird song, or looked at the detail of a leaf (or even the back of your hand)?

We tend to live inside our heads rather than seeing what is all around us, and this influences the way we live. If we are not taking in the right information, then how can we possibly act appropriately? It's a bit like a tree that didn't notice the Sun moving across the sky, and therefore didn't track the light through the day to maximise photosynthesis. While everything we perceive has the potential to enter our consciousness, we leave out much more than we take in. It is estimated that we process a maximum of just seven pieces of information at a time[2] – these might be sounds, sights, emotions or thoughts – so it is vital to have some say in what they are and how we perceive them. That means consciously deciding which senses we use, and when. We need to regularly exercise them all at once to feel life in high definition, and there is no better place to do that than in a natural setting.

Do you remember the awe you felt as a child when the smallest shell on the beach was a marvel to be pored over and treasured? Or when you were first filled with wonder by a startling scramble of woodlice under a lifted stone? Or when you lay staring up at the shapes in the clouds, with your body fully rooted to the earth? There's nothing stopping you from being that child now. Think of a time that you had that sense of heightened awareness, standing in a magnificent landscape. Right at the top of my list is a boat trip I took through the high gorges of Milford Sound in New Zealand, with dolphins swimming alongside, rain pounding down, and tears running down my face at the feeling of never having felt so alive. When you feel this, every sense takes in the experience in ultra-high definition, and you react by feeling exhilaration, with a rush of endorphins and other positive physical reactions.

But you don't have to be in a far-off country – those wonders that we try and emulate when we thrill-seek are open to us whenever we want them. Nature is everywhere – all you have to do is find the wonder in what is around you. To feel fully alive, make all of your senses become fully active, and at the same time tell your mind that it's time to let your senses have a go without your consciousness being in charge.

When you perceive things fully, whether it be in nature or other places, you start to see life differently – you see with fresh eyes. Once you've allowed your senses to take in your surroundings for a while, you can allow your thinking to follow. Your senses will inform your thoughts, and in turn your thoughts will inform your actions. If your senses are dulled, or if what you are inputting into them isn't great, you will find that your actions won't be ideal either. It's 'garbage-in-garbage-out' as the saying goes – whereas what we want is 'information-in-positive-action-out' or 'joy-in-joy-out'.

Your intuition, your feelings and your unconscious senses shouldn't be forgotten. Strangely, studies have shown that our blood pressure rises around conifers but falls around oak trees. This intuitive reaction – possibly triggered by chemical stimuli in the trees' different smells – could be an ancient throwback to times when the safety of different types of woodland was relevant to human survival. Intuition also allowed ancient peoples to navigate vast oceans.

Even now, you and I intuitively respond to the changing seasons by being more active in spring and summer and less active in winter, thanks to our internal senses combined with our body clock. We are less likely to bound out of bed when the sky is dark or grey than when there is bright light shining through the window. When daylight hours are short, our year-round, high-stress culture requires us to work the same hours in winter as in summer, even though our hunter–gatherer ancestors would have changed their routines with the seasons. Some people discover that their bodies revert to their natural rhythms a few days into a camping trip, with sleep and energy patterns that differ markedly from their regular routine. However, what we think of as intuition doesn't happen by magic. In some circumstances it is instinct and in some cases it's learned. I couldn't navigate an ocean right now (even with GPS) but I could learn to do it given enough time, the right teaching and an endless amount of stamina.

'Common sense' is another interesting concept. Often what we see as common sense is actually learned behaviour from the norms of our society. In our modern world, sense is no longer common, so you'll have to decide for yourself. The prevailing view might be that chopping down a tree to have a better view from someone's window, or killing the bees nest in their roof is common sense. Someone might think it common sense to bring a plastic shopping bag to the supermarket, or to buy cheap carb-rich food. However, if the prevailing view was that those actions weren't the norm, or were less accepted by society, then common sense would quickly lead to the opposite action! As with all senses, set aside assumptions, feel your intuition, listen to it, then question it.

So, a word of caution – if you rely too much on what you think intuition is telling you, you may be opening the door to bias, cultural conditioning or incorrect assumptions. When asked about the odds of rolling another six on a dice after five sixes in a row, almost everyone intuitively gets it wrong. In fact the odds of another six remain one in six regardless of how many previous sixes have been rolled, even though the overall odds of six sixes being thrown are 46,656 to 1. Shown the faces of different people we make assumptions (often incorrect) about their character. So I urge you not to succumb to the increasingly popular view that everything you feel inside must be correct.

Why do we have senses? Trees perceive the outer world to give them information to inform them how to act. A tree senses light, then moves towards it, to fulfil the basic need of making food via photosynthesis. We are people, so we have more choice over our senses, but where we choose to direct our attention, and what we observe, informs our actions just as if we were trees. If you focus your attention on something (like a commercial for a sugary drink, for example), your actions will follow (you might feel thirsty, and then buy a drink that's bad for you.) That's why commercials work, by grabbing your attention.

So make an active choice where to look. If you want to learn a musical instrument then listen to more music rather than watching television. If you want to make a difference in the world, go to talks and watch videos of inspiring people. If you want to be fitter, get outside and breathe the fresh air.

When it comes to benefitting from being in nature, don't forget that no-one is selling the outdoors to you. There are no shiny commercials with families enjoying spending time in nature for free (any that do are always selling you something, like a car, rather than the nature itself). Your enjoyment of nature doesn't cost money, so big corporations lack the incentive to persuade you to consume it, and as a society we have fallen for the marketing hype that things only have value when we pay for them. Don't let that put you off. Conduct your own marketing campaign if you want. Direct your senses, your thoughts and emotions towards healthy, natural things – make a glossy video in your head, with the things that you want more of, and experience them in high definition with your feelings and emotions on full power.

Your actions will follow your attention, so be curious and make sure you are looking in the direction you want your mind, your body and your heart to follow.

Case study

Vanessa has a deep relationship with trees.

"Trees have always been important to me. They have provided me with entertainment, interest, security, solace, comfort and – more recently - part of my income.

Growing up in a rambling old stone house surrounded by large beech and horse chestnut trees, my childhood was spent climbing trees (and occasionally falling out of them), swinging from ropes, collecting shiny conkers, roasting chestnuts on the fire, learning about the wildlife that made my beloved trees their home, and building tree houses. And on wild winter's nights, I loved nothing more than to be in my bed, snug under the covers, listening to the mighty beech boughs swaying and crashing in the wind outside my window – the thought still brings me comfort now.

And later, while at university and during my working life, trees and woods have provided me with space to think and a place to be, whether that was lunchtimes spent wandering in a city park with its limes, plane trees and ornamental cherries, the solitude of a Northumberland moor with its stunted, lichen-covered hawthorns, or walking with my dog in a fragrant commercial larch forest."

Be part of the natural world

*"I thought that the trees and the birds belonged to me, but I
realize now that I belonged to them."*

John Lewis-Stempel[1]

Inside us all is a deep and fundamental yearning to belong. Being lonely makes us miserable and on average leads us to live shorter lives. We will do almost anything to avoid it. Feeling connected is a fundamental human need that we actively or unconsciously seek. However, belonging doesn't simply apply to being part of a family or group of people, but to our natural surroundings – we also have a longing to feel connected with the natural world. We might think we are now living in a better world, to which we've become accustomed, but our bodies are telling us otherwise. It's not surprising that being dragged away from the environment in which we evolved is causing us harm. Perhaps it's time to ask yourself if you are suffering from 'Nature-Deficit Disorder', a term coined by Richard Louv in his book *Last Child in the Woods*.[2]

Humans have been modifying their surroundings since their earliest days, but about 12,000 years ago we did so particularly dramatically by abandoning the hunter–gatherer lifestyle and settling down in agricultural communities. From that point onward, we started changing the evolution of the plants and animals around us – for example, when we domesticated livestock and working dogs, and chose only the most productive strains of wheat to propagate. This happened because our ancestors wanted to meet basic needs, such as getting enough food and keeping warm, while avoiding the stress of constantly moving on to follow wild herds or to avoid predators.

Gradually over time, humans became more and more separated from nature, and in the past few decades many of us have been able to live a life almost totally divorced from the natural world, if we so choose. If you don't believe me, think about the number of TV programmes and films that have no nature in them at all (office dramas, sci-fi, reality TV shows, or almost any programme based in a city, to name just a few genres) – we now think this is normal. Technology is making us even more disconnected from living things, and our children play computer games with simulated trees rather than feeling the joy of climbing real ones.

Religious, philosophical and scientific teachings going back many hundreds of years have told us that we humans are at the centre of the universe, above and *apart* from nature, not *a part* of it. And in modern times, in the hugely profitable and prolific self-help publishing industry, there are precious few personal development books that include our living world context. The *Diagnostic and Statistical Manual of Mental Disorders*, the book used by psychiatrists to diagnose mental illnesses, includes only one condition linked to the rest of the natural world – Seasonal Affective Disorder (SAD) – and none at all related to our relationships with our non-human living environment.[3]

The prevailing belief is that nature is untidy and inconvenient – simply a resource to be tamed and controlled. A shocking 96% of all individual mammals on Earth are now humans or livestock,[4] and almost all of the natural world has been shaped for agriculture, resource production, and other human uses.

Oddly, while we are destroying nature at a terrifying rate, we are surrounding ourselves and our children with cuddly toys and online videos of animals doing cute things, so we know that we love nature even when we are separated from it.

E.O. Wilson, the American biologist, set out his theory of biophilia, and defined biophilia as *"the urge to affiliate with other forms of life"*.[5] Research by Wilson and subsequent scholars has shown that we have an innate affinity for the living world, which harms us when it is repressed. It's interesting to ponder that during our evolution we spent as much time interacting with other living beings as we did with our fellow humans – hunting and gathering required it. It is therefore natural for us to have formed strong subconscious bonds with other living things. Our love and need for nature is deep within us, just waiting to be let out.

Of course, when I talk about humans becoming disconnected from nature, I don't mean all humans. Many indigenous societies around the world are still intimately connected with their surroundings. Many communicate with plants and animals, call them brothers, and ask for forgiveness when they kill them. The Pawnees of North America consult animals about the medicinal value of herbs and roots, and revere animals such as bears and eagles. All of this acts as a brake on the exploitation of the natural world, ensuring that resources are available for them and their descendants.

It's common for indigenous peoples to be mocked as primitive and underdeveloped, and for many of us to dismiss the ways of life that have served them for thousands of years without harming the land around them. Similarly, if we want to stand up and express our feeling of belonging to nature, we run the risk of being belittled as a 'tree hugger', 'hippie', 'shaman' or 'pagan'. Finally though, things are changing, with university research on nature connection catching up with what we've known deep down all along.[6]

Making the effort to reconnect with the natural world will always be amply rewarded. It is a mind-shift to suddenly find out that you are part of a huge family of over 60,000 species of tree alone – cousins you didn't know you had.[7] You might not want them to all come round for tea at the same time, but you can experience the warm comfortable feeling that they are playing a supportive and nurturing role in your life. They were there before you were born and will still be there looking after others when you're long gone. You can redefine loneliness when you walk in a wood and feel among friends. The most powerful drug is the promise of belonging, and studies show that the same psychological forces that connect us to other humans also connect us to nature.[8]

For me that place of connection is my garden, where I know everything will be right – where I placed my son in his pram when he was a baby. At that time I was unwell with post-natal depression but I knew that he belonged there, in the sunshine, looking up at the dappled leaves of our maple tree. And his crying stopped.

When you belong, everything seems to fall into place, and rather than feeling insignificant and powerless as you think you might if you've just relinquished your all-dominating hold on everything around you, you instead feel a great weight lift from your shoulders. You feel a rise in confidence, a fall in stress levels, and an immense sense of connectedness, as all the trees in the woodland around you do. So get out and meet those trees, plant your feet firmly on the earth, stick your hands in the soil and get dirty. I urge you to make the effort to reconnect, to feel part of the natural world – it will be worth it.

"We can truly care for nature and ourselves only if we see ourselves and nature as inseparable."

Van Jones

Exercise

Get to know your relatives in the natural world. Do you feel part of nature or separate from it? If you feel separate, examine the cultural and historical factors that have led to this.

Follow nature's patterns

"Nature uses only the longest threads to weave her patterns, so that each small piece of her fabric reveals the organization of the entire tapestry."
Richard P. Feynman

Patterns are everywhere. In the living world, they began when the earliest life-forms started reproducing, and have since evolved into a myriad of different shapes: from the fractal unfurling of a new fern leaf, to the complex neural networks of the human brain. These patterns are not random – they are replicated across the inanimate and the living worlds.[1]

The most accessible example is a branching pattern (which is one type of fractal pattern). Our tree cousins have branches, roots and leaf veins. In the animal world, moles and rabbits create branching tunnels, and in the inanimate domain, stream tributaries combine into ever wider rivers, and lightning branches through the sky. In our bodies we have branching veins, arteries, capillaries, nerves, neural networks and lymphatic systems.

We have the same network patterns in our social systems – friendships, family trees, online social networks, communities and business connections.

Branching networks have evolved for a reason. They are an effective way of growing, covering large areas, and creating multiple opportunities for contact with other things. They stabilise and anchor, and can transfer information, nutrients or other materials efficiently, often in multiple directions.

In addition, networks are resilient. An organism can often lose part of a network and remain healthy. This property was one of the key factors considered by the Federal Government of the United States when it commissioned research that led to the creation of the internet and world wide web. They wanted a system without a central hub, that would be resilient to attack. A hacker or terrorist might bring a part of the network down, but not the whole. You can see the same principle in a tree that loses a damaged branch, and even when an amputee has survived a roadside bomb. Even our brains are constantly pruning unused neurons to make way for others that we will use more.

Woodlands have their own underground branching networks (the wood wide web!) – a mass of mycorrhizal fungi that spread for many miles beneath the forest floor. They transfer nutrients between trees, allowing them to communicate with each other. We'll meet them again throughout this book, so important are they to tree and forest health.

Branches also demonstrate nature's preferred method of getting from A to B – **not in a straight line**. Remember that the next time you set a goal and become frustrated when you are forced to find a way around an obstacle. Straight lines might intuitively seem more efficient, but try drawing a tree with only straight branches and you'll see the problems that arise. Many more branches cross (leading to damage and disease); more head away from the light not towards it (bad for photosynthesis); and others have to turn at sharp angles to avoid another branch (creating problems with the efficient transport of nutrients and causing risks of snapping).

Trees would encourage you to take the wiggly route, which allows for new opportunities as you navigate your way along your journey. Consider a tree root that moves through the soil – its winding habit allows it to seek water on multiple planes, not simply in the soil directly in front of it. And because it isn't fixed on taking a straight path it can wind around rocks that are in its way – and thus not be blocked in its path and not expending unnecessary energy to move the obstacle. By taking a more indirect route you can keep your options open, and you might find the destination you set out toward wasn't the best one for you after all. Examples might be following a career path or business idea that takes a different turn, or widening your criteria when looking for a new partner. The branching pattern allows us to explore multiple opportunities and keep an open mind, without becoming frustrated.

The spiral is another pattern we see replicated throughout nature. We are familiar with spirals in a pine cone, a monkey puzzle branch, a sunflower seed head or a rose bloom. Look closely and you may see a pattern based on the Fibonacci sequence of numbers, a double spiral that has fascinated mathematicians for centuries. Its formation follows a strict numerical sequence, but it occurs in nature because it is an efficient way to pack things into a limited area, and to grow incrementally.

We all recognise negative spirals in our own lives – spirals of negativity, of guilt and of anxiety. How often have you felt anxious, then felt anxious about feeling anxious, making you feel even more anxious! Depression also leads to downward spirals – my experience is that it leads you to withdraw, increasing the sense of disconnection and taking you further away from the people who would support your recovery. Addiction, phobias and eating disorders are similar. You spiral down unless there is an external input to turn things around, like a friend, counsellor, therapist, medical professional or new strategy.

Spirals in nature are laid down incrementally, so the energy input is added only in one position in the spiral at any given time. This is good news because, to bring about change, you have to identify and work on that one particular point, rather than having to change absolutely everything. The challenge is to find which is the right position or the right time to turn that negative spiral into a positive one. That might involve waiting until you have supportive people around you, or conversely seizing a new opportunity right now – only you will know when the time is right.

To know which action to take you might need to look more deeply into the problem. For example, many people in the modern world are stuck in a cycle of unhappiness combined with a shopping habit that neither they nor the planet can afford – they feel unhappy, seek comfort in 'treating themselves' at the shops, then feel guilty (or broke), and ultimately become more unhappy. Then the cycle continues. By realising what the problem is, you can find the sweet spot to break that spiral of unhappiness – in this example by substituting more positive experiences for shopping.

You can harness the power of natural spirals by creating spirals of energy, of confidence, of self-esteem, of action and of happiness. Once you have turned the spiral around, the good news is that momentum keeps it turning in a positive direction, with a smaller amount of ongoing effort.

Our brains perceive patterns all around us – we are hard-wired to spot them. They are shortcuts to accessing more information than we could otherwise take in. When we see a tree, we recognise it from its overall shape, rather than from examining individual leaves and branches. We assume, without seeing them, that it has roots because that's a pattern we've already experienced.

We often perceive these patterns unconsciously. If you are walking in the woods, deep in a daydream or contemplating what to cook for supper, your subconscious will be aware of the blur of a bear or a deer (depending on which country you're in!), and will snap you back into consciousness based on that movement pattern. The same happens when you are driving – if you've zoned out (like we all do), your subconscious will quickly make you aware of another car swerving in front of you. My own pattern recognition can sometimes be a little defective because of the 'brain fog' I periodically experience. I once did not notice a man walk past me dressed from head to toe as a cabbage! Luckily he wasn't a bear about to eat me – I probably wouldn't have lasted long as a hunter–gatherer.

But this pattern recognition survival mechanism comes with a hazard warning. It can lead to a reliance on outdated, rigid or unhelpful thought patterns that can cause us damage. It can also reinforce destructive patterns, such as racism, sexism, and other prejudices that can harm relationships and even destroy whole communities and countries. The challenge of living consciously is to shine a light on thought patterns, to bring them into your mind, and to examine them for what they are.

There are many more patterns that we will explore throughout the book. But the important thing to remember is to make patterns work for you. Trees and all other species use them because they confer benefits, and are effective ways to use precious energy and resources. Use them to **work with nature rather than against it**.

Exercise

Go for a walk in your local park, or in other natural surroundings. Take a photo of each pattern that you see. How can you apply that pattern to your own life?

Engage with the present

*"One of the most tragic things I know about human nature
is that all of us tend to put off living.
We are all dreaming of some magical rose garden over the horizon
instead of enjoying the roses that are blooming outside our windows today."*
Dale Carnegie

Do you sometimes feel that you are watching your life as an observer rather than living it right now? Are you always in 'doing' mode rather than in 'being' mode? Maybe you are stuck in something that happened in the past that you can't move on from. Trees can teach us so much about being present. When you walk past a tree in the hustle and bustle of the city you can see that it is quietly getting on with the task at hand – learning from what's gone before and programmed to consider the future, but not stuck in either. The most important thing is what it is doing right now.

I recently took a group of adults into the woods. The idea was to let go of the stresses of the day and to focus on the trees and plants around us. I had an ecologist and a professional gardener in the group who were already very connected with nature, but they were the ones who couldn't see beyond what they already knew. They were thinking about botanical names, and uses for the different species, but they couldn't see the simple existence of the trees themselves. They were in nature but they were inside their heads the whole time. That is true for so many of us during our journey through life.

I've always lived in the future. That's where my brain tends to go. What should I do next? How should I get there? Why are things not happening quickly enough? It was a revelation for me to find out that other people weren't the same. And I realised how much of the 'now' I had been missing out on. Luckily that was a while ago. I'm still a future person, but now I've learned techniques like mindfulness, meditation and seeking 'flow' (more of that later), that help anchor me to the present moment, while keeping the forward momentum.

Living in the future can also be a barrier to happiness. We tell ourselves *"I will be happy when..."*: when I've passed that exam, when I've landed that promotion, when I buy my ideal car. Of course, when we achieve what we thought we wanted, we move on to the next goal that we think will make us even happier. When we are surrounded by commercials and social media, we can always find something that we think would improve our lot. But of course it doesn't work. As poet and essayist Ralph Waldo Emerson suggested, *"We are always getting ready to live but never living."* Why not give up trying to be happy in the future and learn to be happy now?

Alternatively, some people look at the future only as doom and gloom. It's true that there are many things to be fearful of. However, seeing only the negative possibilities risks leading us to inaction – and trees don't like that at all. They will carry on striving their hardest, regardless of what the future might bring, and they will try to change the world they live in. In the natural world (or as a hunter–gatherer) you don't last long if you do nothing. I can't imagine that our ancestors had much sympathy for the member of the tribe who was perfectly capable of going to find food but instead sat in the cave complaining that the world was going to rack and ruin. That person would endanger the whole tribe. If this sounds harsh, then it is meant to be – if you want a book that justifies sitting around moaning (whether it be on your own, in person, or on the internet) then this isn't it. The world needs people who are alive right now, not paralysed by the future.

Being stuck in the past is arguably even more unhelpful than living in the future. You can at least affect the future, but you definitely can't change what's happened in the past. Thoughts about the past often dwell on regret or missed opportunities, and even happy memories can leave us stuck in our heads rather than being open to the world and what it has to offer now. What amazing wonders and opportunities are missed by living like that?

Tree thinking is being present right now, experiencing what is there, not what is inside your head, and focusing on the activity itself not on what might go wrong. Learning mindfulness is a useful tool that you can draw on at any time. You don't need to be meditating in a group. Learn to bring yourself back to the present anywhere, from cleaning the kitchen floor to walking in the park. Learn to be aware with no judgement. But the real tree way of thinking is to do something productive and focus your attention on it – right here, right now.

Exercise

What does your current mental landscape look like? What proportion of your time do you spend living in the past, future and now? What can you do to shift the balance for the better?

Learn from what's gone before

"Insight is seeing for the first time that which you knew already."

Swami Nischalananda Saraswati

Trees remind us that the past is there to inform our actions right now and in the future – like us, they have 'memories' so that they know what has gone before. Of course they don't have neurons, but they do have a rudimentary memory process that involves encoding information, then retaining the information, then recalling it for use later.[1] Oak trees use tannins to defend against insects, and send chemical messages through the air to other trees to armour up too – amazingly, in the following year, those same trees deploy tannins again without receiving a message, having 'remembered' their benefit from the previous season. (If in future years the tannins are not needed, the trees will ditch them, since the energy used to make these chemical defences could be better spent on other things.)[2]

Another example of memory comes from cherry trees that know to flower in spring (when their fruit has a chance of ripening) because they have retained the information that winter has just happened. They come into blossom when the day length is around 12 hours, but they don't bloom in autumn when the day length is the same. Behind this memory is an epigenetic process that is the subject of ongoing research.[3] Like the oak, the cherry uses this memory to inform its current actions – and the consequence of not remembering would be the devastating loss of its future offspring.

Therefore, the principal thing to learn from trees is that the past is used to know what action to take right now.

So how can we learn from this constructive approach? You may be someone who lives in the past– stuck on times that were better, when you were in a happier relationship, or you felt you were fitter or thinner, or the world was a better place. But all that has passed, and by dwelling on it you risk bringing up all sorts of unhelpful emotions like regret, guilt, and sorrow over missed opportunities or loss. Oak trees can shed their leaves in mid-summer if they are attacked by insects, then grow a second lot – they let part of their past go for the benefit of their future success, and so can you. If there's something in the past that you can't change, recognise that you don't have a time machine, let go and move on. By holding on to past hurt, you are wasting precious energy that you could be using to grow your new leaves and branches.

Actively decide if something that has gone before is productive, paralysing or pernicious to you now. A tree tells us that if it's not productive then it has to go – but you are the one who decides how much to retain, to guide your actions in the future. First, ask yourself what you can learn from it and, if appropriate, how can you make sure it doesn't happen again.

Remember that the scars on a tree never go away. Study any trunk and you will see knots, gashes and holes. Every branch that has dropped leaves a mark. The tree is healthy but evidence of past damage remains. There are remarkable trees that have grown around grenades from World War I, or enveloped bicycles tied to them long ago. Past trauma needs to be met head-on and healed in an active way, just as trees heal over gashes in their branches.

Some of our own scars may never go away, such as those from bereavement, abuse, or the loss of a close relationship, but we can learn to keep on growing, with healthy rings radiating outwards. And we can use our scars as a source of strength, and to help others when they face similar challenges. The concentric circles that we can grow around past hurt are another of the patterns that we see repeated throughout nature (look at your fingerprints to discover a further example).

It's helpful to take a look at your past in an active way. Think about what you learned from your parents, good and bad. John, who provided a case study, told me that he inherited a deep sense of shame regarding his sexuality from his religious upbringing; another a fear of spiders that got in the way of her taking an outdoor job. Examine your habits, beliefs, prejudices, fears and nostalgia. Perhaps some of your existing habits and beliefs are no longer relevant or useful to you now. Depending on what they are, you can tackle them in different ways, such as talking them through with a friend or therapist. One strategy is to develop a sense of stubbornness (as I have – I hate to let anything defeat me). Sometimes all the talking in the world can't replace just deciding to get on with life.

Remember that your recollections may not be accurate and people will always experience the same event differently from one another, like two sisters caught pinching biscuits by an elderly aunt visiting for a family party. One sister might remember the aunt being super scary, while the other remembered that she sent them off upstairs with a little wink.

Be aware that memories remain as feelings as well as thoughts, and emotional memories are often more difficult to tackle. You can consider the origin of your recollections, but it's a waste of precious energy to look for someone to blame, and you may miss an opportunity in the present if you are stuck on '*if only's*' and on worrying about what's gone before.

Once you've been through the active process of considering the past then it's time to switch the frame from then to now. And you do that by asking yourself *"What can I learn from that past experience? How can I use that information now?"*

Did you know that a Venus fly trap has a great short-term memory?[4] It 'remembers' that one of the hairs in its trap has been activated by a fly, but only closes when a second one is touched. The electrical mechanism that controls this works in a surprisingly similar way to our own neurons (nerve cells). In this way, the Venus fly trap conserves precious energy by avoiding closing on flies not big enough to provide a substantial meal – which is important because there are only a limited number of times each trap can close before it dies. This carnivorous plant has a lot to say about using your memories to keep you strong, rather than making you weak. Use your memories to inform your actions and to provide food for your body and your mind.

Case study

Rob, a business advisor and tree-lover, told me how important it is to enjoy the view and to learn from the past to inform the future. I think this wisdom, shared with businesses, equally applies to everyday life.

"Celebrate your achievements. It's so easy to focus on the future and dismiss how far you've come. Every few months, it's a great idea to look back and review your business. What went well? What did you achieve? Were there other things that didn't quite go to plan? What would you do next time to

turn these 'not quite successes' into successes?"

Exercise

Listen to your inner voice. Reframe your beliefs about the past. Turn paralysing and pernicious into productive.

Switch:
—   I wish I had
—   I regret
—   I still feel
—   I can't accept
—   I blame
—   I feel guilty about
into:
—   Next time I would
—   I know I can't change the past
—   I have to accept
—   I have learnt

View the big picture then the detail

"The power and majesty of nature in all its aspects is lost on one who contemplates it merely in the detail of its parts and not as a whole."
Pliny the Elder

When we begin the process of actively observing our lives and our surroundings, we are wise to look without judgement. Not to rush in, but to take time to see what's really going on. When planning landscapes, permaculture practitioners are encouraged to observe a garden or a piece of land for a year. That allows them to see how it is affected by the changing seasons and to decide what they want to keep and what to change. They can also consider the knock-on effects that altering one aspect might have on the others. We can do the same with our lives by stepping back and bringing the whole picture into view.

However, to do so can sometimes be uncomfortable. Life's wondrous complexity can be confusing for us mere humans. We aren't used to the uncomfortable feeling that we can never understand or know everything, however hard we try. Scientists and research establishments in particular try and break nature (including our own human nature) down into its smallest parts, in order to understand it. Those who try to see the biggest picture, the complexity – to see life as it is with all its interconnected elements – have sometimes struggled to be taken seriously. James Lovelock's 'Gaia' hypothesis, is one such example. This hypothesis, set out by biologist Lovelock and microbiologist Lynn Margulis, considers the planet as a whole and explains that Earth is a self-regulating system that maintains suitable conditions for life.[1]

Some qualitative researchers, such as psychologist Brené Brown, have encountered similar problems when studying the breadth of the stories of human emotions and experiences.[2] There has been a widespread scientific view that *"if it can't be measured it doesn't exist"*. Albert Einstein is purported to have a sign on his door that read *"Not everything that can be counted counts and not everything that counts can be counted"* so he was clearly aware of this potential pitfall. Thankfully that is now starting to change, with multi-disciplinary teams bringing different perspectives to the same issues.

Looking at the tiny details in isolation is plainly not the best place to start. If we studied one part of the human genome without any context then we might think we were a gorilla, or even a banana. We might take three notes of a piece of music and conclude that it's by Beethoven rather than the Beatles.

The living world tells us that complexity is good. Nature takes 1 plus 1 and makes 3 or 5 or 79 – there are emergent properties that arise when living things are combined, that can rarely be predicted. If we only look at each element in isolation how can we possibly ever hope to gain more understanding? Both you and a tree are made from the same handful of elements plucked from the same soil and the same air, so it's in the connections between those elements that the magic lies. An apple tree has over 50,000 genes, the most complex plant of all. How can we possibly understand all that, let alone the orchard, the ecosystem, or the planet that it inhabits? We must learn not to be scared of that complexity and to trust in the principles that have kept us and our ancestors alive for billions of generations.

To see the biggest possible picture we must observe the fact that 'life, the universe and everything' works and let go of the need to know exactly how.[3] We should not believe anyone who claims to have all the answers. Most importantly, we shouldn't fill the gaps in our knowledge with stuff that has been made up to fill an uncomfortable void – there are many out there that operate in that space, like conspiracy theorists or those online commentators that write whatever comes into their heads. It is OK to accept that you don't have to know everything

In your own life I would suggest looking at the big things first and only fit the detail into the jigsaw afterwards. Big things might include your close relationships, your meaning in life, your ethics and values. Zoom out to see all your big things together, as if they were lined up on the horizon – ask yourself why are they important? Then start filling in the detail. You might decide that you derive meaning in life from helping others (that's one of your big things), then work out how you are going to do that (perhaps by volunteering with a charity). If one of your big things is having a happy family, find ways of achieving that (more family time, better communication etc). So often we focus on the detail and forget what's truly important.

Overall, try not to focus on irrelevancies and try to keep

things in perspective. When my daughter had a close call after a ruptured appendix, suddenly her leaving towels on the bathroom floor was not so important! Sometimes that big picture comes into view when you least expect it.

Communication is one area where it is very important to take a panoramic approach. Compassionate communication methods allow us to step back and look at a conversation or disagreement in a constructive way that allows for connection rather than division. Normally when we listen to others we load what they are saying with meanings that aren't necessarily there – these might be things we are imagining or worrying about. They might be situations we have come across in the past and are projecting into the current context. Remember that our brains look for patterns to make sense of the world, and may mistakenly apply them in settings where they're not actually relevant. So when we encounter someone saying something that resembles an event we have experienced in the past, our pattern recognition system jumps into action and assigns it the same meaning. For example, if you have experienced rejection as a child you might interpret someone walking away from a discussion as rejection too, even if they were simply needing the toilet! This is one of those circumstances where our human brains can work against us.

Zooming out also gives us an opportunity to examine whether we feel one of our core needs is being threatened and whether we are reacting in an unconscious way to protect that core need. It gives us an opportunity to communicate our feelings without blame. This is sometimes called 'giraffe' communication (compassionate, not taking things personally), as opposed to a 'jackal' approach (defensive, blaming).[4] I like to think of the giraffe way of looking at a situation as being high in the canopy of a tree and viewing the conversation from that distance. I imagine myself up in the branches looking down at everything that's going on, before mentally climbing down to engage with the situation.

In my experience, humans naturally split into two types – 'details' people and 'big picture' people. Both are important ways of seeing the world but have separate roles, and the aim should be to balance the two inside your own mind, with the big picture being placed on the scales first. Each way can be learned by

49

challenging yourself to switch between the two, to bring the two methods into consciousness. When you can combine and apply both types of thinking to the same problem simultaneously then that's the ideal. I am naturally a big picture person – I go for a walk and see a huge landscape, the outline of the trees; but my friend Jane Bevan, an artist who works with natural found materials, sees the tiniest details of a leaf or a seedpod and skilfully incorporates these into her artwork.[5] By foraging with Jane, I have started to hone my skills in looking at the intricacies that life offers, and by doing so I've inadvertently brought those abilities into my life and my work. In my business I value my big-picture brain for planning and strategic decision-making, but looking in more detail means that I am more likely now to spot niche opportunities for growth, or to simply see a mistake on my website. The detail is important, but use it to support the big things. Discover what's important, zoom out to see the bigger picture, and you'll find that everything else will fall into place.

Case study

Alice shared her story. She had a successful career, was super-organised, with a husband and children. Her life ran as she wanted it to and she was very happy. But then her husband had an affair and left suddenly. Her life, unsurprisingly, imploded. During her traumatic and lengthy divorce battle she applied a meticulous eye for detail to every element of the case. But from an outsider's perspective what got lost in the mix were her children, who were of course who she cared about the most. She achieved her financial settlement but saw later that everything had been made more difficult for herself and her children by focusing too much on the detail.

Exercise

Ask yourself whether you are primarily a 'big picture' person or a 'details' person. Can you switch perspective? Can you see the wider context of your actions, such as your effect on other people, other species, and the rest of the planet? Practise mentally climbing to the top of a tall tree and seeing what is around and below you. Try this when you are in a tricky situation, particularly if it is emotion-driven.

Listen to your internal ecosystem

"The quieter you become the more you can hear."

Ram Dass

In his book *The Wisdom of Trees*, Max Adams offers this fascinating description:

"Woody plants are like cities, with bundles of arteries linking production and consumption; power stations collecting and transporting energy; manufactories churning out raw materials and bespoke engineering solutions; communication hubs and invisible infrastructures held in a tight network, fantastically interconnected and unimaginably functioning as a single organism."[1]

He could easily be talking about you. You too are a complex system of interconnected, interacting tissues. Indeed, just like a tree, you are an entire ecosystem. You are full of bacteria and fungi, systems and organisms that make up who you think of as one being. Biologist Lynn Margulis demonstrated that the powerhouses of your cells (mitochondria) originated when bacteria entered primitive cells and began a symbiotic relationship around two billion years ago. Even back then our ancestors were ecosystems, not individuals – and it has not been a bad partnership, I think you'll agree.

Who we think we are takes on a different meaning when we discover that our gut is filled with 130,000,000,000,000 bacteria that keep us healthy and help digest our food. You might want to say thank you to them next time you eat your lunch, or flush them down the toilet.

Unfortunately, we're often at war with our own ecosystems, inside as well as out. Antibiotics may save lives but they kill off the 'good' as well as the 'bad', making them a blunt tool for the treatment of minor illnesses. Think twice about those antibacterial sprays, as they are implicated in the rise in allergies as we isolate ourselves from dirt, rather than playing in the soil that contains natural antibiotics to keep our bodies in balance. Creams and lotions upset the delicate mix of organisms and cells that help keep your skin healthy – there are more natural alternatives, and the overwhelming majority of the plethora of products on our shelves can be avoided altogether.

Sit quietly and listen to what your body is telling you. Your diet, sleep patterns, exercise and rest all have an impact on how you perform. Many people are sleep-deprived and have sleep patterns at odds with their natural cycles. Are you a night owl or a lark? Are you an adult working night shifts, or a teenager staying up all night to play computer games? Sleep deprivation is a physical problem, but mentally it's a killer too. (Parents take note, it does not contravene their human rights to take phones away from teenagers at bedtime!)

If you listen hard enough and often enough, your body will tell you what it needs. Don't try and kid yourself that what you want and what you need are the same thing. I told myself for years that the odd glass of red wine was good for me (I happily latched onto the studies that supported that), although my body was crying out for me to stop drinking. You may find that what is good for other people is not right for you. Do your research but remember that you are unique, just like every tree in a woodland, and you will have to find your own balance.

Listen to your own early warning signals, such as stress, anxiety and those quiet (or not so quiet) voices in your head that say slow down! We see anxiety as a bad thing, but that uncomfortable feeling has a message, and that message is not to run away from the problem but to sort out whatever is making us anxious, whether it be external (like a relationship or work challenge), psychological (like a past experience rearing its head), emotional (like a fear of failure) or physical (through illness, diet, sleep or other factors).

Feedback mechanisms exist in nature and in ourselves to keep things in balance. When the temperature goes up and a tree increases its transpiration rate through its leaves to keep cool it is adopting a feedback mechanism similar to your body when it sweats. A stimulus warns that conditions have moved away from the ideal situation, and a reaction is triggered that helps bring conditions back into balance. When your unconscious and conscious brain gets involved, things start getting complicated. Your body is giving you feedback all the time, but you have to learn to listen to it and not keep overriding it (like the last time you ate dessert when you already felt full, or stayed up late watching TV even though you felt shattered).

Emotions and thoughts have purposes. They are calls to action. Keep your channels open, scanning for them, acknowledge them and then decide what to do with them. Even deciding not to follow through on an emotion or a thought is a positive action and frees up more of your precious energy for other things. But remember that so-called 'negative' emotions are useful too, and the challenge is to learn to use them, not to be reduced by them. Anger and guilt can be great motivators if you can turn them into helpful action. Positive thinking is fantastic – it can take you a long way – but you're not being realistic if you try and be that happy positive person all the time. Throw a pity party now and then!

Finally, knowing your mind is an integral part of knowing your ecosystem. It takes effort to know who you are and how you operate. It's a tough process to look at yourself in the mirror with a compassionate yet analytical eye, but it's important to continue to do so throughout your life. Become self-aware of your thoughts, emotions and actions. Look at yourself and also your interactions with other people, seeking out those subtle feedback signs that other people offer, like body language, sounds and silence, and look with a compassionate heart towards them and towards yourself.

There are barriers to self-awareness, such as fear, stubbornness, and family and cultural background, but don't let the fear of emotions hold you back. Some people are born with less natural self-awareness – but several people who are on the autism spectrum are the most self-aware people I know, because they have put the effort into knowing themselves and the way their brain works. Self-awareness can be learned by all of us.

Remember that your ecosystem is a complex one, but your mind can be an active participant helping to bring it back into balance.

Exercise

Keep a 'biotime' diary, recording your diet, exercise, energy, mood, health and how much time you spend outdoors. Take what you've learned and use it to inform your future actions.

Group 2 Principles

Purpose

Live with purpose

"Nature does nothing uselessly."

Aristotle

Finding a purpose has been shown to be the secret to living a happier, more fulfilled and longer life. That's not really a surprise when we look at how trees' strong purpose drives them on, keeping them healthy and resilient.

For a tree, life may be hard, but purpose is easy – growth, reproduction, ensuring the survival of offspring and contributing to the survival of life in general. But what about us? If our health is compromised or food is scarce, then that becomes our priority. For many of us, children and family are the centre of our world. But if our core needs are met, what then? We still need to fill our days, and find meaning for life.

Often we feel that our purpose is to be successful – but what is your definition of success? Does it align with the definition most of us, as part of the industrial growth society, were brought up with – concerned with wealth, money, fame, status, and being better than others? Or with a tree's definition, which is about growth, vitality, resilience and co-operation? Power is often a driver for success, but is it 'power over' (others) or 'power with' (others)? Martin Luther King Jr. defined power as the ability to achieve our purpose and effect change – quite different from the power that has the potential to corrupt politicians, business leaders, and every one of us if we're not careful.

If we bring our purpose back into line with what we observe in the natural world, we don't have to discard the benefits of modern life, but we can leave behind many of its destructive forces. Defining your purpose in terms of growth, learning, support, nurturing, collaboration, creativity, abundance and progress – without being restricted by rigid goals – decouples you from feelings of failure, poor self-worth, lack of direction, and guilt at not being the 'best'. Forests would never define what they do and where they are going in the same dysfunctional ways that we do, and they would never punish themselves or others for not achieving what is expected.

Longevity studies on locations around the world where life expectancy is exceptionally high ('Blue Zones') undertaken by author and explorer Dan Buettner have found that purpose is worth seven extra years of life and that retirement is positively dangerous without it.[1]

In Japan there is a concept of *Ikigai*. Roughly translated it means what makes you wake up in the morning, your reason for being – and it doesn't have to be a big thing. A grandmother of 100 may find her *Ikigai* in sitting in a chair watching over her grandchildren. For others, *Ikigai* might mean running a successful company, following a profession that is a calling, being an athlete, musician, artist, craftsperson or writer. *Ikigai* is something you feel, not simply do.

So, how best to find your purpose? Living with purpose is about living a certain way of life, not about the end result. The sweet spot is to find something you love (you'll get a win–win dopamine hit in the process); something you're good at; and something the world needs. If you can make a livelihood from it, then that's the icing on the cake. But don't feel that your purpose necessarily has to be found in your job. Maybe it's promoting sport for local kids, or supporting refugees, knitting woolly hats for premature babies, or engaging in wildlife conservation in your local green spaces – it will be personal to you. My hope is that you will discover your purpose in making the world a better place (more about that when we explore the principles in Group 6). Purpose is not a one-off activity, it's a thread that runs with you and propels you forwards from whenever time in your life that you discover it.

Next explore your values. These are your core inner beliefs. You can't adopt anyone else's – not your parents', your friend's, or your faith leader's – you have to find your own. Values range from love, kindness, honesty, justice and co-operation to adventure, challenge and creativity. Turn on your emotional barometer (feel, don't just think) in order to find out which are really important to you and let that spur you on. Find what makes you come alive. Values will act as your anchor throughout your life, bringing you back to what's truly important. They will get you through even the hardest of times.

Ethics are next – look at what you are doing through a lens. Are you living and making decisions by considering how to care for yourself, care for others, care for other living things, and care for the health of our living planet as a whole? These are questions that trees never have to ask, because for them playing their part in creating abundance never needs to be questioned, it just happens.

If you live according to your values and ethics then you are well on your way to finding success and happiness in life. Happiness is something we all seek, but chasing it will only make it more elusive, so don't set it as a goal in itself. Find what is right for you, and happiness and joy will be side-effects on your journey.

Finally, the most important factor in finding fulfilment is to discover meaning outside of yourself. This involves focusing your attention away from looking inward at yourself, your own life, cares and concerns, but instead to look towards external factors, such as other people and the wider world. As psychologist Mihaly Csikszentmihalyi states:

"I think that evolution has had a hand in selecting people who had a sense of doing something beyond themselves."

I believe that's true of our tree cousins too. We'll discuss thinking beyond yourself and being a guardian of the future in the last group of principles.

Now is the perfect time to make a change – to actively find the purpose that will propel you onwards, enabling you to weather all kinds of emotional and physical troubles along the way, and you will find yourself super-charged with energy you didn't know you had, to achieve things you perhaps had never even dreamed of.

Exercise

What makes you come alive?

List the values that are important to you. Can you use those values to find your purpose?

Don't stop growing

"If you really want to eat, keep climbing.
The fruits are on the top of the tree.
Stretch your hands and keep stretching them.
Success is on the top, keep going."

Israelmore Ayivor

The odds of a beech nut becoming a mature tree are around 1.8 million to one. Having made it past the squirrels and the other creatures who might eat it for breakfast, it has to hope it has been deposited in a fertile spot, with enough rain and warmth to start the germination process. Once the little shoot emerges there's no going back – it has to grow with all its might. It will not give up, through the sapling stage, being battered by the wind and browsed by animals, struggling for light and striving, with the hope of one day becoming a mature tree. It won't produce its own nuts for 80–150 years, and will carry on growing for many hundreds more. When times are tough it will probably try harder – when light is scarce it will reach upwards towards it; when the wind is strong it will put down stronger roots. I gain inspiration from this beech tree, knowing that life takes effort. As author and activist Helen Keller said:

"Life is a daring adventure, or nothing."

We humans are different – for us positivity is a choice. We can choose to brave the odds and keep going, to be the best that we can be, or we can give up, deciding it's not worth the struggle or that we're bound to fail. But despite the differences between us and that beech tree, achieving our goals involves the same simple formula that nature offers our little beech nut. First work out where you are now; next, work out where you want to be; third, work out what you have to do to get there; and finally, do it! This is great advice from David Taylor as set out in his book *The Naked Leader.*[1]

Experts offer various approaches to goal-setting. Some say goals should be realistic and match our skills to opportunities. Others say set huge goals on the edge of achievability and that way you will always achieve more than you would have done otherwise. I tend towards the latter. After all, you can always gain new skills to get where your purpose is propelling you. Some realism is a good idea though. Don't believe the self-help gurus who say you can do anything or be anyone – try turning into an oak tree and see how far you get.

What's certain is that if you want to live a fulfilled life then doing nothing, or indulging in learned helplessness, is not an option. How many of these voices do you recognise?

> *"It's not worth the effort."*
> *"It probably won't work out."*
> *"I don't want to get hurt."*
> *"I'll look stupid."*
> *"Someone else is better at it than me."*
> *"I haven't got the skills."*
> *"I have no natural talent for that."*
> *"I've tried before and failed."*
> *"Nothing less than perfection will do."*

Are any of these internal (or external) voices holding you back – stopping you from plugging away like the beech nut, the sapling, or the mature tree?

Most goals don't have to be big – it's really the journey that counts – and you can break tasks down into manageable chunks, as long as they are part of your overall vision. It's good to examine your limits, but mainly focus on where you want to go and what you need to do to get there. Evolution and instinct work for the beech tree, but we, as humans, must think about what we want to achieve.

Don't shy away from effort. Mindset psychologist Carol Dweck was spot-on when she said:

> *"Effort is one of the things that gives meaning to life. Effort means that you care, that something is important to you, and you are willing to work for it."*[2]

Make a plan for success, like giant oak trees do. They have 'mast' years, when they produce masses of acorns with the hope that some will escape being eaten. They build up nutrients from the previous season, and then go all out to achieve their goal.

Of course, oak trees never know whether their efforts have been rewarded, but usually we, as humans, can benefit from seeing the fruits of our labours. In my experience, there is no better feeling than the satisfaction of achieving something you've set out to do – something that fits squarely within your purpose and values. As I often say after the long tree planting days in our community woodland, when we've hosted hundreds of people to plant thousands of young trees, *"I love it when a plan comes together"* (a somewhat cheesy quote from the 1980s TV show *The A Team*). At the end of the day, exhaustion miraculously becomes a source of energy, and I feel revitalised by a sense of achievement. Furthermore, because that activity falls squarely within what I feel as my purpose in life (making the world a better place) the hit of exhilaration is off the scale.

Whether your goal is running a marathon, or simply getting dressed if you are feeling depressed, the effort will be worth it. And it will feel even more rewarding if the achievement involves helping others, like raising money for charity, or getting out of bed to have coffee with a friend who is also living with mental illness.

The principle *'don't stop growing'* also encourages us to continue learning throughout life. Our oak tree learns to work around obstacles, and to re-grow after a lightning strike. Nature is constantly finding innovative new ways of solving problems, being creative in pursuing purpose. Your equivalent might be to take an evening class or an online course, read books and watch fascinating documentaries. I love online courses, especially those that make complex subjects accessible in bitesize chunks. Becoming learning-orientated rather than results-oriented will also make you happier, and finding ways to absorb information with a critical eye will free you from the agendas of media editors, politicians, friends, and online writers.

Remember, too, that most of the adaptations and efforts that trees make are done by **'action learning'** – learning by doing. They try something, they get feedback, they adapt and they try again. The adaptations aren't always the best, they often don't work out, but they may be **good enough** to move forward.

The message from them is to get stuck in and give it your best shot.

So go for it and don't stop growing!

Case study

Sunita described to me how trees can inspire confidence to keep someone motivated in a business context.

"A lofty ash standing tall and proud seems to me to be exuding confidence. For many small business owners, confidence can be an elusive trait – 'Imposter syndrome' may strike at any time or we have our own personal mind monkey sitting on our shoulder chattering into our ear and undermining any confidence we may have. However, when we have a vision and know our purpose, the 'why' of our business, we can set attainable goals that are aligned with our non-negotiable values to take our business forward. When we know where we're going and what the next step is in getting there, we can speak confidently at networking events (after all, we now know why we're there!) and we can be sure that whatever path we eventually take, we're heading in the right direction. We can hold our head up high and move forward."

Exercise

List the steps you can take to keep growing towards your goals.

What sources of learning can you access?

Learn self-regulation

"As human beings, our greatness lies not so much in being able to remake the world as in being able to remake ourselves."

Mahatma Ghandi

The biggest feat of self-regulation occurs at the level of our entire planet. Individual feedback mechanisms exist within every organism, but each individual is also interacting with others around it, creating a dynamic whole. These relationships ebb and flow, and the process is so well established that billions and billions of organisms dance together to bring the whole world ecosystem back into balance. It's a feat of chaotic brilliance.

There are two types of feedback – balancing feedback (sometimes rather confusingly called negative feedback) and amplifying feedback (known as positive feedback).

In balancing feedback, a sensory input tells the system that conditions have moved away from the ideal state, and then an action is triggered that brings the system back to the required equilibrium (which might be in the same place as before or a different place). This is how trees regulate the amount of water in their leaves. An example from your own body occurs when the weather gets hotter and your temperature rises, kicking in your temperature regulation system which brings your temperature back down to normal.

The other type of feedback – amplifying feedback – magnifies an outcome. So, for example, when an apple ripens, it releases ethylene, which triggers neighbouring apples to ripen and release their own ethylene – and so the effect grows (the apples sniff each other, ripen and pass it on). A human example of amplifying feedback happens during childbirth. When a contraction occurs, the hormone oxytocin is released, which stimulates the hypothalamus in the brain to produce more oxytocin, which increases both the intensity and frequency of the uterine contractions.

Amplifying feedback loops almost never continue unabated. As environmentalist Donella Meadows explains:

"Positive feedback loops are sources of growth, explosion, erosion, and collapse in systems. A system with an unchecked positive loop ultimately will

65

destroy itself. That's why there are so few of them. Usually a negative loop will kick in sooner or later.'[1]

For us, self-regulation means taking responsibility for ourselves and our actions. Some self-regulating behaviour is instinctive (for example, pulling your hand quickly away from a dangerous heat like a fire), while some is learned (for example when a child discovers they should listen while someone else is speaking). Learning to be independent – to be able to direct your own path through life – is one of life's greatest treasures, so avoid being overly reliant on others, in order to develop your own strength and confidence.

Much of our modern life has removed the balancing feedback mechanisms that would allow us to be healthier and happier. Addictive foods and poor eating habits (like eating at your desk or in front of the TV) override the body's natural feedback mechanisms that should suppress appetite. Alcohol and drugs can mask psychological or emotional signals that would identify an underlying problem and allow possible solutions to be found. Internet trolls don't have the self-regulatory mechanisms provided by a group of friends at the pub telling them not to be such idiots. Increasingly, we believe that we have the right to be heard and not challenged, so the traditional checks and balances on discourse are removed.

On a grander scale, media outlets often present only one side of an argument and we are now able to self-select our preferred echo-chamber and forfeit the chance to hear different ideas in favour of the ego-boost of perpetual reinforcement of our own views. This leads to a potentially dangerous polarisation of ideas and perspectives, rather than a healthy balance of free speech.

Emotions play a strong part in self-regulation. Listen to them – they are all useful, regardless of whether we label them as positive or negative. They are telling you that something needs to change. Dig deep and explore the causes, not the symptoms. What you discover will ensure that your actions are appropriate. Anger could be due to frustration or lack of confidence, or even a lack of food or sleep. It might be linked to something that's happened in the past. For example, I realise now that the bullies at whose hands I suffered in school were themselves damaged people externalising their own problems. It's a shame they weren't challenged to look at their own behaviour and supported to make the necessary changes to their own lives.

Happiness is a call to action too – to do more of the thing that is making you happy! (as long as it is healthy for you, those around you, and the planet). We all have emotions, so don't be afraid to share them – you will not be alone if you open up and explore them with an open mind and a willingness to address anything that arises.

I am wary of self-help books that tell you to 'be yourself'. That seems like a get-out-of-jail-free card to do whatever you want. Try and be the best self you can be, given the resources and situation you have. That's what our tree cousins do – try their hardest with the opportunities they are given. A baobab tree might find itself in the middle of a desert, but the fact that it has less water than other trees won't stop it from trying its hardest.

Changing your mindset and 'who you are' seems scary, and it takes a lot of effort. I embarked on that process in my early twenties when I looked in the mirror and decided that I wanted to make changes. Eventually I managed to ditch most of the negative thinking, the self-criticism and blaming other people for how I felt; and am so much happier, more productive and more pleasant to be around than I was back then. Of course it is a constant process that takes ongoing effort but, in my experience, is well worth maintaining throughout life.

If this is something you are trying to do, be kind to yourself in the process and don't beat yourself up. Give yourself top marks for trying. It is dangerous to aim for perfection; **nature doesn't do perfection** – any tree will show you that – but you can aim for good enough. Ask for support in the process; you need others to give you realistic and supportive feedback that stops you spiralling downwards.

How does self-regulation relate to our efforts to raise happy and successful children? A child who is not allowed to make any decisions or mistakes is being denied the opportunity to grow and develop self-reliance. Our modern world encourages parents to be fearful, seeing dangers around every corner, and we are unwittingly raising a generation who don't know what it's like to have a grazed knee, let alone play out on their own, or come home covered in mud after the type of adventure I used to have as a child. My brother soon learned to test the strength of a branch after one snapped under him in the tree he was climbing and he ended up in the neighbour's garden (no harm done). I gained in self-confidence after my pony and I were charged by a curious herd of cows. (Word of advice: shouting and waving your arms around is highly effective in repelling inquisitive cattle!) Luckily the pony was unfazed. These two examples show how 'bad', as well as 'good', experiences can teach us valuable lessons. Children benefit when their parents are realistic about the relatively small risks, and balance them with the benefits that being outdoors brings.

Forest schools are fantastic at encouraging children to discover the line between risk and safety for themselves. For example, children are allowed to use knives and saws to make wooden items, so when they grow to be teenagers (a naturally risk-taking time), they've learned that risks come with consequences.

For children and teenagers, testing the boundaries involves carrying out an action, seeing what the result is, then modifying the action next time – it's a feedback loop, just like those that trees use to grow and adapt. A child who seeks their parent's attention may test how their parent will react by having a tantrum. If the response is that they receive a lot of attention, guess what happens: self-amplifying feedback (more challenging behaviour!). The alternative is to give positive feedback for the behaviour you want to encourage – sending that spiral in a positive direction.

On a societal level our feedback mechanisms have gone to the extremes of amplification. To have a healthy system we must balance short-term and long-term needs. We must judge when it's better to delay our satisfaction for the greater good of ourselves and of others. However, we have created an industrial growth system which values only short-term goals, so now the world's entire economic and social systems are engaged in self-amplifying feedback at every level. Consumption breeds consumption by creating needs we didn't have. Long-term goals are impossible for businesses beholden to shareholders, or for politicians with four- or five-year terms of government. Elections could act as self-regulatory processes (many constitutions and international treaties are designed for just that), but with limited numbers of political parties all working under the same system, the electorate has few real choices. The destruction of the natural world, poverty, inequality and epidemic levels of stress and ill-health are the result. As historian Theodore Roszak explains in his book, *Voice of the Earth*:

"We currently find ourselves somewhere at the outer limit of a particularly exaggerated oscillation. It is called urban-industrialism, the wilful withdrawal of our species from the natural habitat in which it evolved."[2]

It makes me sad and angry in equal measure when I hear people say that humans are parasites and that the natural world will eventually come back into balance once humans are extinct – and they imply that this is a good thing. I don't doubt that we humans are on a dangerous trajectory, but why resign ourselves to extinction when we have the know-how to live very differently?

It's important to remember that there are people living in the twenty-first century in ways that are not exploiting nature. The Sentinelese Islanders of India, the Yanomami tribes of South America, and the Inuit of Canada are co-existing with and mutually dependent on other living beings, not standing over them. We, in the 'developed' world, may not wish to live in remote tribes, but there are attractive alternatives to how we live now, as we will see later in the book. We must heed the Chinese proverb that states:

"If we don't change our direction we're likely to end up where we're heading."

None of our self-regulatory tasks are easy any more. We have never been further removed from our tree cousins' way of living – balanced by natural mechanisms, over relatively short timescales. However, I believe that our wonderful, creative, problem-solving brains can play a central part in bringing our incredible planet, and our own lives, back into balance.

Exercise

Choose one area of your life that you would like to regulate in a better way — such as sleep, diet, confidence, self-esteem, anger, emotional reactions and so on.

List the steps you can take to bring yourself into balance.

Catch and use energy effectively

"The lofty oak from a small acorn grows."

Unknown

All living things are ultimately powered by sunlight. Trees and plants extract carbon dioxide from the air and, via photosynthesis, turn it into the life that exists on our planet. Catching energy is their number-one priority. Trees have found thousands of ingenious solutions to meet the challenge of harnessing the power of the great ball in the sky.

A mature tree can have 350 km^2 (135 square miles) of solar collecting cells (chloroplasts), packed into a mere 490 m^2 (5,274 ft^2) of ground. Laid side by side they would cover an area four and a half times the size of my local city of Nottingham! Some fit their leaves together to form a tight canopy, moving with the Sun. Young deciduous trees try to get a head-start in spring, opening their leaves in the very short window before their parents shade them. The reverse happens in autumn, when they wait for their parents to drop their leaves and take the opportunity to play out in the sunlight for a little longer. The sunflowers in my border stubbornly turn their heads to the south as they track the Sun throughout the day. The koatree in Hawaii and the British holly are remarkable in that they have two types of leaves, so they capture energy effectively in shade and in full sunlight. Trees have complex 'vision', so they can perceive light, its direction and intensity. In short, trees and plants have come up with thousands of ways to make best use of the energy source shining from afar.

For trees, sunlight is a scarce resource that must be used as efficiently as possible. Conversely, in the modern world, humans tend to think of energy as being without limit. We flick a switch and there it is. In fact, most electricity comes from burning 300 million-year-old sunlight in the form of oil, coal and gas – but it's so universally available to us that it's easy to squander and devalue. The irony is that sunlight is effectively an inexhaustible resource, but we feel that solar and other renewable energy resources somehow limit our activity. On the other hand, fossil fuels are severely limited, but they make us feel that we

71

have endless power. No wonder we have such a hard time breaking our addiction to them.

So what can we do to catch energy efficiently on a personal level? Our energy comes in the form of food, so we are wise to consume the best range and quality of food that we can. Consider increasing the proportion of plant-based foods in your diet. Why use enormous amounts of energy (not to mention water and other resources) on converting plants into meat by feeding them to livestock animals? If you do choose meat as part of your diet, explore the different meat options and farming methods, such as organic and grass-fed. Changes to diet and agricultural practices account for many of the top ways to reduce global carbon emissions, with a plant-rich diet coming in at number four in a recent study of the top ways to lower CO_2 emissions.[1]

Storing energy effectively also comes from sleep, rest and mindful activities. Exercise also has the potential to leave you feeling energised, especially over time as your fitness increases.

Friendships and other relationships are like a hydroelectric power-station-sized source of renewable energy, so make sure you are investing in them! Like a tree that moves its branches with the sunlight, bend towards people who 'energise' you.

Try to think of your energy levels as a bank account – remembering to always remain in credit. Make sure your energy-level bank account has a wealth of deposits (such as nutrient-rich food, rest, and stress-busting activity) so that if you need to make a big withdrawal (maybe a stressful project at work, or a physically demanding holiday), you won't go badly overdrawn, and your body (or mind) won't give up. This method is how I keep on top of my own fatigue, which is a side-effect of my immune-related illness. Chronic fatigue involves a breakdown of the functioning of the mitochondria (the powerhouses of our cells, which make energy available for life processes). Since tree cells have mitochondria too, I wonder if they ever suffer from chronic fatigue? Something to research perhaps...

Remember to **focus your energy where it can have the most effect**. Think of trees concentrating their branches at the top of the canopy, rather than wasting effort lower down. When I became ill I didn't have any energy at all. I lay in bed all day, and when I did get up I invariably overdid it. I was so happy to be feeling vaguely human that I tried to cram everything I needed to do into the day. That made me feel good, but the next day I would crash and be worse than I was before. Eventually I realised that I needed to balance my energy more. Using my energy where it could have the most effect meant saying no to lots of things; it meant pacing myself; and it meant balancing the chores with the fun things so I could still enjoy life. Learning from the ways trees use their energy wisely, I no longer feel lazy for doing less or guilty about saying no.

However, even when you ration energy you can achieve great things – as artist and author Julia Cameron says:

"Sometimes using tiny amounts of focused energy can move mountains, whereas masses of unfocused energy would not move a single stone."

A similar principle is to design for **maximum long-term yields with the minimum overall effort**, as nature does. Usually that involves greater up-front effort (like when a tree puts on a growth spurt to reach up to the canopy) but with longer-term savings (the same tree will then need to grow less quickly in the long term, thanks to that initial burst). This is totally the opposite of what our *"I want it now"* culture demands – short-term hits that satisfy a superficial need, or taking the path of least resistance. When raising children, this might mean not giving them whatever they want right now, with the belief that they will grow into better people (and may even appreciate you when they have their own children!). That requires some feats of willpower when they come home saying all their friends are allowed to stay up late or have the latest gadget. The same is true for saving for retirement, or planting a fruit tree that won't bear fruit for several years.

Finally, remember to **manage your energy, not your time**. That's tricky in our modern world that works on linear time rather than the daily and seasonal natural cycles that our bodies evolved with. Energy naturally fluctuates throughout the day, so try to make the most of the times when you have energy, and actively slow down at the times you don't.

If you have a job where your workload forces you to work so many long hours that it's making you sick, it's time to step off the rat race. Doing so can be scary – but you don't need to be a

73

millionaire to make that change. Ask yourself if you can thrive with less (don't aim merely for survival, be creative about what living a fulfilling life means to you). The money that you earn is only the tip of the iceberg of the resources you have access to, such as your own creativity, your family and friends, bartering, growing your own food, and the savings made from leaving behind a consumer lifestyle. Harness those sources of energy and you won't need nearly as much money to make your world go around.

Exercise

Create your own energy bank statement. Put deposits down the left-hand column, and withdrawals in the right-hand column.

Deposits might be: good food, sleep, rest, leisure time, enjoyable activities, physical exercise (if it energises you), breathing exercises, mindfulness, healthy treats, time with friends etc.

Withdrawals might be: family commitments, work, chores, strenuous leisure activities, exercise, unavoidable late nights, occasional 'binges' etc.

List the things you do to make the deposits outweigh the withdrawals.

Find slow and small solutions

"Nature doesn't hurry, yet everything is accomplished."

Lao Tzu

When we talk about slow solutions, yew trees, Britain's longest-lived species, come to mind. They can take 100 years to reach sexual maturity, spending the time beforehand putting down strong roots. The soil, wind and rain will influence their growth, but, in general, slow growth means denser wood, more resistance to pests and disease, stronger roots, and less chance of breaking in the wind. Slow-growing box trees have rings incredibly close together, making theirs one of the most dense and highly prized woods. But the record for the oldest and slowest-growing trees must go to one quaking aspen colony in Utah in the USA, which covers 106 acres (43 hectares) and is around 80,000 years old. This, the world's heaviest organism, has one giant root system and 40,000 stems that are clones of each other!

It's interesting that most synonyms for 'slow' in the dictionary have negative connotations. I believe it's time to re-evaluate our relationship with time, especially when we consider that evolution has taken life 3.8 billion years to get where we are today.

Trees are patient – take the lodge pole pine. Its cones stay on the tree for decades waiting for fire to destroy its competitors, which gives its seeds a head-start in the cleared, post-fire soil. We may equally find we must wait for years until the conditions are right for us to really germinate into who we want to be. Have patience – it will happen if you don't give up.

Whether it be crash diets versus healthy eating, working long hours versus work–life balance, credit versus saving, intensive workouts versus building exercise into your daily life – slow solutions are more effective in the medium and longer term.

What about small solutions? Does size matter? Did you know that 99% of species on Earth are smaller than a bumblebee – they certainly don't think it matters! In modern life we are sold the dream that bigger is better – the desire for a larger car or house leads many people to buy on credit they can't afford. Lessons from the 2008 economic crash are all around us, but sadly our society is back to the same dangerous levels of debt.

Small solutions use fewer resources, benefitting everyone on a finite planet. Many trees, of course, do not remain small, but they must balance the risks and benefits of growing big, and keep their growth gradual and strong.

Small also means local. It's incredible to think that trees, even those with enormous height and spread, transport everything they need over a distance of just a few metres – water, nutrients, energy from sunlight – and they do this with amazing efficacy. However, our own ability to move ourselves, and move goods, leads the UK to import large amounts of butter while exporting similar quantities each year – that wouldn't pass the tree definition of efficiency.

By buying locally you are supporting an economy that puts money into the hands of people near to you – a shopkeeper who pays for a maths tutor for his daughter, or a farmer who doesn't have to give almost all of her profits to a multinational supermarket, thus saving enough to take a well-earned vacation. Talking of vacations, is a plane necessary for yours? I'm sure you can find beautiful places to explore within easier reach of home.

Slow and small means dialling back the complexity of life. I believe that we have too many choices and temptations in our modern lives, but the more possessions we have, the more hassle they are to maintain or replace when they inevitably go wrong. It's a vicious cycle that causes us an ever-increasing amount of stress. While living in the woods of Massachusetts, nineteenth-century philosopher Henry David Thoreau wrote:

"Every morning was a cheerful invitation to make my life of equal simplicity, and I may say innocence, with nature itself".[1]

We can all take measures to simplify our lives, the easiest one being to not buy anything that you don't absolutely need. That way you don't have to deal with breakages, replacements, waste, garbage, clutter (or guilt). If you feel you will be tempted to buy unnecessary items, don't visit shopping centres and instead find alternative ways to spend your time.

One slow and small solution is *Hygge* – a Danish concept – a feeling of cosiness or charm, and of creating moments to appreciate the time you have right now with present company. It might be an open fire, or a deliberately made cup of coffee, or a night in with friends. These are purposeful acts, to bring something special into your life. You can't buy *Hygge*, you have to create it.

Learn to appreciate what you have and find pleasure in the simple things. When I was very ill, my diet was reduced to around fifteen different foods. I had previously been a foodie, but I learned to find pleasure in my cup of coffee and get excited at creating a new recipe combination with such a limited range. Not able to go out, I found a warm bath became a luxury as great as any trip to a spa. Now that I feel better, these still have the same pleasurable associations. Having less, rather than longing for more, makes you feel happier because you can experience the pleasure in everyday things.

One proven route to finding happiness on a regular basis is to **seek out 'flow'** experiences. Researched by Hungarian-American psychologist Mihaly Csikszentmihalyi, flow is that feeling of being in the zone, doing something productive, where you focus your attention to the exclusion of everything else.[2] To experience flow you have to be good enough at your task and you must engage fully with what you are doing, free from distraction. It might be sport, dance, knitting, yoga, Tai Chi, playing an instrument, or painting. It might occur in your job (repetitive but challenging factory work even has the potential to be a flow experience). My greatest flow experiences come when gardening. One of my most pleasurable activities is potting-on seedlings, and I love pruning trees too. These are repetitious exercises where all feeling of time disappears for me. The marvellous thing about flow is that it has knock-on effects into the rest of your life, increasing happiness and lowering stress even after you've finished the task. My theory is that plants, in tune with the natural rhythms of life, have flow experiences (although not conscious ones). Plants and animals respond to the moon, the flow of the tides, the passing of the hours, and the changes that the seasons bring.

My guess is that our hunter–gatherer ancestors had many everyday flow experiences while gathering berries or following the tracks of animals (*"Don't distract me, I'm in the zone, man!"*) but now we must make a conscious effort to integrate these into our lives. I would certainly advocate gardening as a flow experience and of course it can have the added benefit of growing healthy food too. I wonder if flow is one reason that gardeners have been shown to be happier than the general population?[3] If we are to transition to a better way of living, many more people will be needed on small-scale farms, so I believe we should design these positive experiences into the work from the outset. There are certainly more opportunities for pleasurable (and skilled) flow activities on small farms than in monotonous industrial agricultural work.

All around the world there are movements encouraging us to slow down and re-localise. The 'slow food' movement that started in Italy in 1989, and has since spread around the world, celebrates local food cultures, promotes the enjoyment of quality food rather than 'fast food' (which is often consumed 'on the go', and frequently contributes to the stress of life). Local currencies (such as the Brixton pound and the Bristol pound in the UK) are currencies that can be used in local independent businesses (and in the case of Bristol used to pay local taxes). Local currencies are used in addition to the national currency and have the great benefit of keeping money in the local economy, creating a multiplier effect that is lost if money is spent in national chains. 'Slow fashion' arose as an antidote to 'fast fashion' (which encourages cheap, poor-quality clothing that often quickly ends up in landfill). Slow fashion values quality garments, designed to last, in addition to vintage and hand-made clothing. 'Slow food' and 'slow fashion' create an emotional and cultural relationship with sustenance and clothes – items that we usually take for granted.

The construction of houses from local renewable resources (such as straw, clay, mud or sustainable timber) has been practised for millennia, and is now seeing a resurgence in popularity. We recently constructed a roundhouse classroom and meeting space in our community woodland, made from local straw, clay and timber.[4] It is a beautiful organic building that is prompting an emotional response from many people who visit. It's time to create more buildings, clothes, food and other items that we can fall in love with.

Slow parenting is also important. If you can, after school, sit down for a family meal round the table, followed by reading books or playing games together, instead of rushing children from one club to another every evening. You will benefit as well as the kids. We worry now that any time not spent engaged in homework, sport or other activities is time wasted for children, but they need time to switch off, or to be allowed to be creative without screens (this might prompt a few cries of *"I'm bored"* before they find something to amuse them, but hold your nerve!). They can develop their imagination, creativity and problem-solving abilities during unstructured time.

Facilitate conditions so your children develop at their natural pace, nurturing them while not stunting their growth. Often children are pushed to the next 'milestone' (academic or developmental) when they aren't ready and will reach their potential in their own time. Be inspired by an ash tree parent that closes its branches to limit the light to its offspring, helping it to grow slow and strong.

Finally, it's important to realise that, while slow and small solutions are the aim, **change can happen in an instant.** Trees put in extensive groundwork underpinning their great releases of energy, such as when they burst into leaf in the spring. One of the longest to prepare for 'action' is the talipot palm, which flowers only once at 30–80 years old, but then distributes hundreds of thousands of seeds all in one go.

The concluding message from trees, therefore, is to have giant aims, occasional bursts of energy, but to use slow and small solutions to get there.

Exercise

What steps could you take to slow down and re-localise your life?

Can you incorporate 'slow food' and 'slow fashion' into your lifestyle?

Make a list of simple things you find great pleasure in, or could incorporate into your life.

Value your uniqueness

*"In a forest of a hundred thousand trees, no two leaves are alike.
And no two journeys along the same path are alike."*

Paul Coelho

Take a walk in a birch plantation among rows and rows of birch trees, and you'll see them all planted in lines, all identical with their glistening white bark. Look again – of course they are not identical, but our brains are used to seeing in patterns, grouping similar things together to make sense of the world.

It is remarkable that no two living things on this entire planet are the same, and even genetically identical clones, such as banana trees, grow up differently – thank goodness, or the world would be a very boring place. In nature, diversity confers health, growth, creativity, vitality and resilience, so it makes sense for you to see your own uniqueness as being of the highest value.

You have evolved to be unique, but live in a society that tells us that we should all conform to the same ideals of beauty, all think in the same way and own the same things. We are told to aspire to be like others, whether it be friends, neighbours, celebrities, models or millionaires. But this way of seeing ourselves is making us ill as we move further and further away from being valued as individuals and towards being valued only for how we look or what we own.

When raising children, it's important that we (as parents, family members or teachers) encourage them to believe in themselves and their abilities. Take them on a walk in the woods and explore how each tree is unique. Let them feel each tree's gnarly bits and bendy branches. Each bend or scar represents an experience that makes them what they are. We love trees for their character, and that should be the same for people too.

There is **no such thing as 'perfection'** in nature. It's an entirely human construct. The more of us that stand up and say we are proud of our size, our scars, our wrinkles and our hair colour, the more young boys and girls will have the confidence to step out of the shadows of prescriptive advertising, blogs and photoshopped magazine images. Shout your 'imperfections' from the rooftops!

Being imperfect is good for relationships too. Connections are made by showing vulnerability. When my daughter was small, I made friends with a mother who came to the school gate fully made up, with hair beautifully blow-dried. I, by contrast, rarely managed to drag a comb through my hair. I felt that I couldn't possibly have anything in common with such a perfect-looking mum. But when we sat and had a coffee one day, she confessed that her looks came as a result of an acute lack of confidence. She was actually envious of me and my willingness to go out looking like I'd been dragged through a hedge backwards! The fact that I was comfortable with how I looked allowed her the space to feel vulnerable and make a connection. And her vulnerability meant that I was given a window into her world of low self-esteem, and could empathise with her as a result.

Physical disability, mental health, chronic illness and neuro-diversity should also be viewed through the lens of valuing the individual. The medical model of 'disability' suggests that it is the person with the disability who is abnormal, but the social model says that our surroundings are the problem and that they can and should be adapted to meet a wide variety of individual needs. Disabilities often confer benefits, such as the ability to empathise, to be focused and to value what's truly important in life.

Society has a very narrow definition of 'normal' mental landscapes too. Fortunately more and more people are speaking out, not only about their own struggles, but about the unique insights that mental illness gives them. The different ways that our brains work gives us our individual creativity, strength and personality. By reaching for the antidepressants so willingly, I fear we label every mental difference as a problem and an illness.

Neuro-diversity means we all have unique ways of thinking and of processing the world – let's celebrate that, rather than be too quick to assign labels, or reach for pills as a 'cure' for being different. In children, the number of prescriptions for medicines to treat ADHD and other associated conditions is skyrocketing.[1] As a society we seek to medicate children while simultaneously making them live in environments that restrict natural behaviours such as being able to run off energy, to play, to **'go wild'**. A study by the UK Office of National Statistics published in January 2018 showed that children aged 8–15 spent an average of just 16 minutes per day in parks, countryside, seaside, beach or coastal locations.[2] The same study showed that children enjoyed their time spent outdoors in these locations significantly more than time spent indoors. The number of hours at school sitting at a desk have increased, and playtime has decreased, so no wonder kids are struggling. Forest school (outdoor learning that encourages creativity, confidence-building, teamwork and problem-solving) has proven benefits for children. In my local primary school we created a school garden, to be used as a venue for learning, play and confidence-building, not simply for growing food. We witnessed great benefits for all the children, but particularly those with behavioural difficulties. A 2005 study in by the American Institutes for Research reported a 27% increase across a range of measures (from science skills and classroom behaviour to co-operation), for sixth-grade students who experienced an outdoor education programme.[3] The most successful programmes are those that encourage an exploration of the child's unique talents, build self-esteem, and develop practical and emotional skills.

I often ask myself why humans seem to have the urge to tidy everything, from backyards to houses to large landscapes. Our neighbour cuts down his native hedges each year to keep them tidy, then puts a birdfeeder in his garden, having decimated the bird's nesting spaces – an irony and a tragedy. On a grander scale, Capability Brown, the eighteenth-century English landscape designer, moved whole villages, had acres of lakes dug, and planted trees in particular spots in order to 'perfect' nature. Think of the energy saved if the lords and ladies of the manor could have appreciated our beautiful natural landscape. The poem 'Inversnaid' by Gerard Manley Hopkins evokes the desire for wilderness:

What would the world be, once bereft
Of wet and of wildness? Let them be left,
O let them be left, wildness and wet;
Long live the weeds and the wilderness yet.[4]

So leave untidy places in your garden and your home. Throw away those magazines that show 'perfect' homes with clean lines. Lighten your burden of possessions, but leave room in your life for creativity, which is messy. Just as nature would, spend your energy on doing and making rather than tidying – **leave wild spaces** in your life – places for spontaneity and creativity, where magical things can happen.[5]

Many of us have favourite trees that we love regardless of their contorted ways. I love to look at the hollows and scars of mine as a reminder to value how I am different from other people, rather than allowing myself to be laid low by insecurity.

Finally, remember – you are unique, you are imperfect, and you are also part of a whole forest full of wonderful diversity. As author Maya Angelou so aptly said:

"If you are always trying to be normal you will never know how amazing you can be."

Exercise

List your unique characteristics, such as your talents, your looks, the ways you think, the ways you interact with others. List advantages (not disadvantages!) for all those characteristics.

Use your edge

"He that will enjoy the brightness of the sunshine
must quit the coolness of the shade."

Samuel Johnson

The most fertile and abundant spaces in nature are often found at the edge between two ecosystems – for example where dense woodland and open grassland meet. Diverse species benefit from the combination of sunlight and protection that edges bring.

One way to consider this principle in your life is to think of your own edge as the edge of your comfort zone. Stay where you think you are safe and you may avoid uncomfortable emotions such as anxiety and fear of failure, but you will also be robbing yourself of some of life's most exciting opportunities – possibilities for new experiences and for self-discovery. Allow yourself to be vulnerable and to take the path that winds through the forest edge with no end in sight. Tell your inner mental critic to keep quiet for a while. It may be whispering that if you try, you are bound to fail – instead ask yourself what you would do differently if you knew you would succeed.

I find that the best way to approach leaving your comfort zone is to 'just do it' – no messing around. It's likely to be uncomfortable (that's why it's called a comfort zone), so you just have to launch yourself off, as if you were jumping out of a plane (which actually I did, years ago, so I speak from experience). Finding out that you don't die if you do something you're afraid of is a good way to learn – whether it be skydiving, or giving a speech at work. There is only so long your body can keep pumping out those stress hormones until the feedback balancing mechanisms kick in.

Laughter helps when you try something new – try taking up something you know you'll be terrible at, like a new type of dance, or a new art form – although laughing in a life drawing class might not be appropriate! Remember that not everything will work out – you have to be prepared for feeling rubbish when things haven't gone how you'd hoped. Organise a 'failure' party, and congratulate yourself for having had the courage to give something your best shot.

One technique that works well for exam and presentation nerves is to envisage your feelings of fear and anxiety as excitement. The two emotions may seem to be opposites but they have similar physical symptoms (elevated heart rate, dry mouth, butterflies in the tummy, and so on), so telling yourself you're excited is more effective than telling yourself not to be nervous. My daughter tried it for her final high school exams and it worked!

Using your edge also encourages you to be a pioneer. Someone has to be the birches and alders of this world, colonising uncharted territory, while others, like oak and beech, follow. Birches were the first to arrive in Britain after the last Ice Age, swiftly travelling northward as the ice receded. Pioneers love the sunlight out in the open. They are a vital first part of the process of creating a diverse ecosystem in which many others can survive. Where would life be if individuals didn't have the courage to move into new spaces and find fertile niches?

There is a wonderful TED Talk called *How to start a movement*, which includes a video of a guy dancing in a field with loads of people sitting around.[1] Then the first follower comes, stepping outside of their comfort zone, and transforming the 'lone nut' into a leader. Then more and more people join in, and eventually it is the people sitting down who are in the minority and find themselves wanting to fit in. It takes courage to be the first, or the second, or the third, but when you take that leap you will also find others doing their own expressive dance, in the same field or another one nearby. Birch trees aren't alone in their colonising journey – they have alders and cherries alongside them, and they work together and draw on support when they feel lonely.

When anyone asks me what my favourite tree is, I say the birch, because it seems to live in that area of discomfort, knowing that a better world has the potential to be created. The 'birch-me' is surrounded by a fabulous bunch of like-minded others working together, but it still feels like it's waiting for the rest of the world to catch up with the ideas that would enable great change. At this moment in time I feel that millions of people around the world are holding their breath looking around to see who is going to be the first to act – the first to dance in a field. The global political, economic and ecological scene is full of uncertainty, and right now we do lack high-profile leaders. But the mainstream media don't show that there are already millions of people taking action, in big or small ways. Like the birches, cherries and alder trees, they have discovered the fertile new ground and are willing to share it with everyone else. If you are a pioneer please don't give up. Hold your nerve and wait for the tipping point that will create an unstoppable momentum towards great things. If you are lucky enough to know a pioneer wanting to make the world a better place, in whatever field, then have the courage to be one of the followers that will help turn a 'lone nut' into a leader or a lone birch tree into a vast woodland.

Make yourself vulnerable, take risks – feel the discomfort and do it anyway. That's the way to create a new life full of opportunity.

Exercise

Do something to put yourself outside of your comfort zone. Hold a 'failure' party if it doesn't work out! Then pick yourself back up and try again.

Group 3 Principles

Surroundings

Create ideal conditions to thrive

"Plant seeds of happiness, hope, success and love;
it will all come back to you in abundance. This is the law of nature."
Steve Maraboli

We are all products of our environment – the physical manifestations of the interactions between our genes and our living conditions. We have that in common with all living things. Our genes get turned on and off depending on what's going on around us; our minds and our bodies are soothed, battered or otherwise altered according to what life throws our way.

When you are born, you already contain all the basic ingredients for survival: physical – like the ability to breathe and to digest food, and instincts – such the sucking reflex and the urge to bond. But where you happen to be born, or in what circumstances, is the result of chance. An acorn that gets eaten by a deer and later deposited within a fertilising heap of droppings is off to a better start than one that lands in the bare shade directly under the tree. In human terms we call that 'privilege'. If you have been born with that healthy heap of fertiliser then it's right to be grateful and gracious, using your head-start to respect and support others.

As adults we have choices with regard to our surroundings. We can recognise that our environment is a good one and doesn't need changing; or we can choose to adapt to what we have; to modify our situation; or even to leave it behind. Our final choice would be to remain in an unsuitable environment without adapting, modifying or moving – not a good idea. (In fact in evolutionary terms the latter would eventually lead to extinction.) Looking at our surroundings in this way is an active and ongoing process as our circumstances and our environment change over time.

This is what Darwin was referring to when he spoke of *"the survival of the fittest"* – he meant that organisms which are better adapted to their environment are more likely to survive and reproduce. Logically, then, if you can adapt to or modify your environment to match your needs more closely, you have a better chance of thriving.

Trees don't simply adapt but actively modify their environments. Willows stabilise the soil along rivers, by putting down long roots; woodlands lock moisture into the ground; and forests of trees warm the air, helping all the plants growing there to avoid frost damage. Coastal redwoods in California can add up to 30 cm of water to their immediate environment in one summer, by condensing fog on their leaves, which drips down to the soil below, creating their own humid microclimate. We see the ways that forests modify their environments in a devastating way when they are cut down – the result is loss of moisture (in the soil and the air), soil erosion and flooding.

Working together, trees in forests create rainfall, alter flows of warm and cold air, and regulate light and shade. Did you know that without coastal forests pushing moisture inwards there would be no rain further inland than 400 miles?[1] As James Lovelock said in his book *Gaia*:

"living organisms have always and actively kept their planet fit for life".[2]

To create ideal conditions in your own life, first examine where you are right now. Suggestion number one – 'if it ain't broke don't fix it'. Forests don't actively set about radically altering things when they don't have to. For example, they can create abundant life with minimal turning of the soil – unlike conventional agriculture with intensive ploughing, resulting in soil erosion and nutrient loss (see Group 6 principles for alternative agricultural methods).

Dan's story illustrates the ways we should look at where we are now, before making radical changes. He told me of his mid-life unhappiness. He had a stable marriage, independent children, and the successful career he had always wanted. But when the opportunity for an affair came along, he was tempted, yet couldn't even put his finger on why. He had everything he wanted so why was he even considering the risk of throwing it all away? Fortunately he identified the need to talk to his wife, and see a counsellor, about how he was feeling. Sometimes when we think we need to make changes it may be more effective to find ways of appreciating and tweaking what we already have.

However, if you do identify an area of your life that really is not serving you then be active about fixing it. Perhaps you feel it would help you to eat less junk food, or use fewer products containing potentially harmful chemicals. Maybe you want to rethink your career situation, or work on a relationship. If there are multiple areas for improvement, pick one thing as a starting point and work from there.

Perhaps start with an easy win that could have a big impact – for example, are you surrounding yourself with toxic substances, from face creams to chemical-soaked upholstery? It's not difficult to ditch them, paring down to the less toxic necessities, such as a few natural toiletries or beauty products, and just one or two plant-based cleaning products (and spending the savings on a treat of your choice!). When I started getting sick as a teenager in response to my surroundings, someone told me I was 'the canary in the coal mine' – they meant that I was one of the first to react to everything around me and that I was an early-warning sign for others to see what damage modern life (1980s style) was already doing. Thirty years later, hundreds of millions of people around the world are reacting to the harmful toxins that are everywhere in our environment and in our bodies. Most won't be as unlucky as me and react in an extreme way to everything from food to chemicals, medications, creams and cigarette smoke, but if you are one of the growing number of people who feel that living this way is not good for you, then it's not difficult to make some changes immediately.

Actively look at your home, your job, your workplace, your leisure time and decide whether they are giving you what you want. Match your surroundings to your goals. If your goal is to compete in your first 5-mile race, replace all the junk food in your cupboards with healthy snacks. If you want to go for regular walks, it's best not to have the television as the focal point of your room. The layout of your house can radically alter how you spend your time. If you can, make your dining table a central feature – it will improve your eating habits, and also become a social space and a venue for creativity.

To be healthy, in body and mind, to find inner peace and calm, head to the countryside, and nature will do half of the job for you. However, if you don't have access to wide open spaces, you can grow your own natural environment – for example by creating a sanctuary in your garden, if you have one, or a community garden in your local park, or encouraging your employer to renovate their outdoor space so it is inviting and pleasurable to spend your lunch hour in.

Try the **100% in nature challenge** – this is something I have devised for my course participants and readers. Challenge yourself to design your life so you can see or be in nature 100% of the time. Walk to work via the park, put a pot plant on your desk, grow some vegetables, plant a window box, walk in the woods, climb a mountain, buy locally grown flowers, run in the park rather than at the gym. At your child's school, bring back the nature table or help to create a garden where the children can learn to grow food. Create beautiful sensory spaces at your local hospital or residential home for the elderly. If you're struggling to quite get to 100% of the challenge, fill the gap with paintings of nature on your walls and nature programmes on television, or wear clothing in nature-themed fabrics. These can also be enjoyed if you have a disability or chronic illness that prevents you getting outside as much as you would wish.

However, just as we can look to trees for inspiration about creating ideal surroundings, we can also look to them for warning signs. They are suffering from pollution, toxins and destruction of their ecosystems just as we are, making them more vulnerable to pests and diseases. We must urgently listen to what they are telling us about changing the environment in which we (and they) live. You can play an active part, since creating ideal conditions for your local trees to thrive will result in the same benefits for you and your family.

As a species we humans became well adapted, over tens of thousands of years, to all the diverse environments on the planet. So it makes no sense to destroy the ecosystems that we're adapted to live in. And don't get me started on the idea of abandoning Earth and looking to live on other planets. The first challenge of inhabiting another planet will be growing green stuff! Let's value the green stuff we have here instead.

For yourself and your family, making changes big or small will require energy, but once you have created your own personal and family microclimate, it will pay dividends and create positive spirals that keep it on an upward trajectory with less ongoing effort. Your hard work will be rewarded if you create your own ideal conditions, inside and outside, inspired by the forests that have established the environments necessary for the survival of life on planet Earth.

Exercise

Take the **100% in nature challenge**. Modify your living conditions and your daily routine to aim to see or to be in nature 100% of the time. This will take time and careful observation but don't give up. More ideas for the challenge are given at the end of the book.

Find your niche

*"Don't assume you are on the right track
just because it is a well-beaten path."*

Unknown

When I go for a walk I love to discover all the different places that life calls home. You can find trees living in cracks in concrete, on cliff edges, on waste ground and in water. You'll even find shrubs growing in the branches of trees, like the Christmas favourite, mistletoe. Trees provide millions of niches for different types of life. An oak is home to thousands of species of plant and animal, and if you sit quietly you can observe each tree in a forest as a city, with each creature having its own place within the whole.

But what about us as people? You'll find your niche in life by knowing that you are unique, so set aside any ideas of unquestioningly following others. Find what you love and set yourself the challenge of developing it. Don't be put off by not being an expert. The word 'amateur' comes from the Latin word *amare* (to love) – be someone that loves what they do, and does what they love. Don't forget that Albert Einstein was an amateur physicist (he worked in the Patent Office). Be aware of your limits and of how much you still need to learn, but you may have to stand tall and project confidence, even when you don't feel it.

Imposter syndrome may occur when someone feels like they don't belong (usually in a job). They may have actually found their niche but can't appreciate that they belong there. A tree doesn't suffer from such self-doubt (another benefit of having no brain!). You'll find it helps to acknowledge your (misplaced!) sense of being a fraud, talk about it (many other people suffer from the same feelings), and try to re-frame the doubt in a more positive way. You might tell yourself that you can't know everything but will improve over time. Remember that nature demonstrates the benefits of 'imperfection'.

Finding a niche may involve entering a competitive field, yet discovering a unique opportunity within it. While nature will find opportunities for colonising new ground, in reality there are few areas of the globe uninhabited by plants and animals. Indeed these existing areas may be places where there are greater opportunities to thrive. To find where you can maximise your opportunities, offer something different from, and over-and-above that which everyone else is offering. An example of this is a fig wasp who will find a safe space to lay her eggs inside the unfertilised 'fruit' of the fig (cosy cups where her young will be protected and have a food source). In return, she offers a pollination service. There are more than 750 species of fig, and incredibly there is a different species of wasp for each species of fig – over generations each wasp has developed a symbiotic relationship, finding its niche in a crowded market. A human example might be a wildlife photographer who enters a competitive field but specialises as the best photographer of fig trees, or of wasps!

Remember to provide niches for other people too. This could be by supporting others to create livelihoods, by taking on employees, or being a collaborative partner. Some of the most exciting creative spaces are innovation hubs where different people share workshop or office space and spark ideas off each other. The venue provides the niche, and often the more diverse the disciplines of the individuals collaborating, the more creative the ideas and innovations that result.

Of course your niche doesn't have to be in a job – maybe it's pursuing a hobby. A friend, Abbie, makes costumes for the local drama school, using her sewing and crafting skills and gaining enjoyment from watching the kids perform dressed in her (sometimes wild) creations.

You can help your children find their own niches in life – they might not be what you would like, or expect them to be, but it's ultimately up to them. Support them until they are independent enough to thrive on their own, but avoid being over-protective – finding their own niche will involve risk as well as rewards.

If you have already found your niche, that's great! Make the most of it and congratulate yourself on your achievements. But eventually you might find you risk becoming stuck in a rut – if your niche was a good one but is now boring or no longer giving you a challenge, set yourself a new goal. Explore new opportunities with fresh eyes. You might consider moving to pastures new. It's a common belief that trees and plants can't move, but try telling that to the brambles in my forest garden who regularly 'walk' around, reaching their tips into new openings in the canopy, where they can grow greener and stronger out in the sunlight.

Remember that conditions will change. A competitor enters the market, or technology moves on, your personal circumstances change, and you may have to shift your niche. Adapt or move on, but always make your niche your own.

Exercise

What is your niche? Perhaps you have a niche at work, in your free time, in your family or community. Perhaps your niche is intellectual or creative. Do you need to take action in order to find or create one?

Invest in your wellbeing

"Your heart is full of fertile seeds, waiting to sprout."
Morihei Ueshiba

If trees were conscious of the human world, they would recognise the importance of the wellbeing industry that is seemingly everywhere right now. Yet they would think it strange that wellbeing is not already built into our daily lives. Trees set about establishing ways to truly flourish – their ultimate aim is to be as healthy as possible so they have the best chance at reaching their potential. They seek out rare minerals, necessary for health and long-term survival, such as nickel and molybdenum (don't you just love that word?), as well as abundant ones such as nitrogen. Birch trees survive freezing by actively pushing potentially damaging air pockets up through the tubes that transport their sap; and some pines have anti-freeze in their leaves so they can retain them in winter. Pine trees in frozen climates thicken the undersides of branches, which means they don't snap with the weight of snow. All of these adaptations help to keep them healthy and help guard against future problems.

The World Health Organization definition of health is:

"a state of complete physical, mental and social well-being and not merely the absence of disease or infirmity".[1]

For we *Homo sapiens* that means actively investing in our wellbeing in a wide variety of ways – ensuring that our physical, psychological, emotional, intellectual and social needs are met. In the first group of principles, we looked at observing our own ecosystem as the first step, but now we can get on with making a plan for wellbeing. Sadly, we can't expect wellbeing to be automatic – especially not in our modern world where so many different elements, like poor-quality food, stress, nature deprivation, toxins, and consumerism conspire against us.

First, let's look at modern medicine. I'm a big fan – it keeps me alive on a daily basis and saved my daughter's life. My son wants to enter the medical profession. However, I do think modern healthcare systems could equally be called ill-health systems, treating us when we are already ill, often dishing out pills rather than long-lasting therapies. Talented doctors have limited time to listen to their patients and can only scratch the surface of complex health issues. In my experience, many specialists seem reluctant to consider illnesses outside of their particular discipline or specialisation, both in the medical profession and also in the field of complementary medicine. I visited numerous doctors and complementary therapists over the years and I found that almost all believed *their* diagnosis, treatment or specialisation was 'the one and only'. When they couldn't find the root cause of a physical symptom, they jumped straight to mental health, previous trauma (of which I had none), imbalance in my chakras, or anything else they could think of that couldn't be disproved. It was only by taking active steps myself to improve my wellbeing that I finally worked out the diagnosis and the regime that was right for me.

In my experience the best person to know your own health is you, so start with getting to know yourself, and then recruit medical professionals and complementary therapists to work for you, designing your own 'garden' full of supportive elements. Seek a diversity of solutions rather than just one.

Try to ensure that as many as possible of the activities in your life have the added benefit of supporting your wellbeing – for example, by finding a job that brings you pleasure, or taking up a hobby that involves, as a side-effect, exercise, healthy eating or relaxation. Who you spend time with can make a difference too – if your friends or partner enjoy healthy activities, they will be a good influence.

If you try something new, like a therapy, diet or activity, be systematic about changing one thing at a time, so you can assess the results for yourself. That way you are more likely to stick to the changes that bring improvement and discard the ones that aren't working.

Wellbeing can be cheap or expensive, it's up to you, but you might want to consider making your health and wellbeing a priority over spending on other items. Can you really afford that new pullover, but not that osteopath appointment or health class? Having said that, the people who live longest around the world spend almost no money on keeping fit and well, having a daily routine that is free, and that keeps them healthy.[2]

Wellbeing strategies also include those of protection and prevention – willows use salicylic acid to deter pests, for example. There are many safe ways you can protect yourself, with preventative medicine, herbal remedies, nutrients, vitamin D (the sunshine vitamin), and prebiotic foods, for example.

It's difficult to avoid fast food and processed food, but the only strategy I know that works is to make a commitment to say no to it – we all know that poor-quality food is at the root of many of our modern illnesses, like diabetes and heart disease to name but two. Modern soils are now lacking in many minerals, since agriculture has depleted them and only replaces the main NPK (nitrogen, phosphorus and potassium) nutrients by means of synthetic fertilisers. Grass-fed meat and organic vegetables (preferably home-grown) are best if you can get hold of them, because they're grown in more nutritionally complete soil, and therefore contain more of the trace minerals you need for good health.

You might also feel that certain types of foods, such as gluten or dairy products, may be causing you harm. If you do eliminate foods, be systematic and keep a diary to record the changes you make and any changes in your symptoms. Consult a qualified nutritionist.

In general, a well-balanced plant-based diet will protect you from all kinds of illnesses, and increase your lifespan. One way to establish a great deal of diversity in your diet is to create a grid with 50 squares and in one week try to eat a different food for all 50 squares (don't count the same ingredient twice – bread and pasta both primarily contain wheat, for example). Not only will *you* be getting a wide range of nutrients but you'll also be nourishing that inner ecosystem of beneficial bacteria that you share your body with.

It may come as a surprise that people who live the longest rarely undertake formal exercise.[3] Movement and activity are part and parcel of their daily lives, such as gardening, tending animals, walking to the shops or visiting friends. This accords with a tree's approach to activity – energy is expended as a means to an end, and never as a purpose in its own right. Consistent activity woven into your daily routine is many times more likely to be continued over decades, with the consequent long-term health benefits.

Wellbeing also refers to investing in your need for protection, for example from emotional stressors or troubled relationships. However, don't put up barriers beyond those that are needed. If you've been hurt in a previous relationship then it's natural to be fearful, but those emotions may ultimately harm your chances of finding love again. Lower your defences when the time is right, like the camelthorn acacia that puts cyanide only into its young pods, but makes them attractive to giraffes when they are mature. (Not that I am suggesting that anyone's ex should get a dose of cyanide!) Take advice from the neem tree, which uses an insect-repelling chemical in its leaves but not its flowers, so as not to repel the insects it needs for pollination. Make sure you are repelling the people you don't want around but not those you need to let in to give you the support you require.

Breathing effectively may appear to be the most fundamental requirement of life, but we can discover new techniques to regulate the amounts of oxygen and carbon dioxide in our system, and lower stress levels. Yoga and meditation are particularly effective for learning the various methods of breathing for different circumstances, such as getting off to sleep or coping with stressful situations. One simple method is to sit for five minutes making your out-breaths longer than your in-breaths.

Finally, believe that you are worthy of being looked after. Value yourself and remember that wellbeing is a journey, not an end result.

Case study

Inspired by trees, Charlie shared great advice for keeping healthy.

*"**Drink plenty of water.** This wisdom was given to me some years ago by a travelling storyteller from Wales who handed me a card that shared lessons from trees. I now look at these giants and think how much water they must drink to keep themselves healthy. Obviously, keeping hydrated by drinking plenty of water is essential for your brain to function effectively, but to maintain your resilience and be able to cope well with challenging situations you also need to make sure you eat healthily, get enough sleep and take regular exercise – maybe a walk in the park at lunchtime or a run*

through the woods after work. And don't forget to take some time out – the sky won't fall down if you switch your emails off for the weekend! There's often no boundary between work and life, so it's easy to look after everyone else – your clients, your family, your children – and forget about yourself."

Exercise

Put together a wellbeing plan. Change just one thing at a time and keep a diary to track the results.

Spend a day in the outdoors discovering the ways that nature can support you with your wellbeing.

Plan for each need to be well supported

"Even if one tree falls down, it wouldn't affect the whole forest."
Chen Shui-bian

What are your needs? Maslow's famous hierarchy of needs suggests that physical needs must be met first; next are the needs for health, safety and freedom from fear; then love and belonging. Self-esteem and respect come next; then knowledge and curiosity; and then beauty in art and nature. Finally there is the need to realise your full potential. I would put the need to connect with nature closer to the more essential end of the scale myself, but you get the idea. To be resilient, a living thing should have more than one way to meet each of these needs – the number may vary but aim for at least three ways for each.[1]

The idea that **each important need should be supported by several different strategies** is based on sound methods employed by each and every tree – for example when they seek to satisfy that most basic of needs, for water. A beech tree employs multiple water optimisation strategies. It can cause its branches to droop so as to direct rainwater to the ground closer to its roots; the lignin in its trunk prevents it drying out; it has shallow roots in the fertile forest floor to catch the rain before it can be poached by other plants, and it makes friends with fungi to transport water underground. A mature tree can take up 200 litres of water per day, and if there's a drought, it can employ additional strategies to meet the demand, such as using its taproots to bring water up from deep underground.

Around the world, trees have hundreds of ingenious water collection methods, depending on their circumstances. Baobab trees in dry regions of Africa store thousands of litres in huge trunks, growing and shrinking according to the season. The dragon's blood tree catches mist in its leaves and shades its roots to prevent evaporation. And in southern Africa, the mopane has leaves shaped like butterflies that close up to prevent water loss. Evolution has clearly selected for the trees that meet this basic need in multiple ways and according to their own individual environments.

103

Meeting fundamental needs in multiple ways applies to your own need for love and belonging. This need could be met by just your partner, but what happens if your relationship breaks down suddenly? People who are happier tend to have six to eight good friends that are with them for significant parts of their life – so cultivate several good friendships and invest in them.

Your psychological health can follow the same rule of three. These can be underpinned by friends, *and* by professional counselling when needed, *and* by strategies such as mindfulness and breathing exercises.

Keeping fit and active might be maintained by walking to work, *and* going to a fitness class, *and* tending your garden. That way, if you can no longer afford the gym membership you've got it covered in two other ways.

Your income needs will be more resilient if you have more than one earning stream, so if one job or contract comes to an end you have others already in place. This is called a 'poly-income lifestyle'. In modern life we are taught to specialise in one thing, but that's not what nature does; that's what Henry Ford invented for his factories! Before industrialisation every person would have had multiple roles on top of their regular job – for example, the local blacksmith would have helped with the apple harvest (and have been paid in cider, lucky him). In hunter–gatherer days everyone had multiple roles – part gatherer, part hunter, part cook, part child-minder, part entertainer, part builder, part fire-tender and more. Societies were much more equal as a result, because each member was aware of the challenges associated with every task, and could empathise with the others.

Many artists and craftspeople I know have poly-income lifestyles that involve making and selling work, giving talks, working in schools, and teaching workshops for adults. This gives them the flexibility to put energy into the areas where the financial income and their interests lie. Their livelihood can adapt to their needs, their commitments and their stages of life. And having more than one income stream means that if work in one area dries up, they have others to compensate.

Similarly if you run a business or are self-employed, 'tree-thinking' would encourage you to develop multiple markets rather than relying on just one. For example someone running a plant nursery might sell from the nursery gate, attend shows, have online sales, and seek corporate clients to whom they can sell their wares.

Raising happy and fulfilled children can also be achieved with a poly-input approach – from parents and step-parents, grandparents, wider family, teachers, activity leaders and friends. Having more than one person involved definitely makes life easier – for example, when they're very young it's a lifesaver to be able to hand a screaming child over, or to have someone to bounce ideas off. There are fantastic groups for lone parents with support, shared activities and diverse role-models. The more adults that are involved, the more likelihood there is that a child will find someone to confide in, or someone who has time to give them some extra attention or help with their homework, for example. The old saying that *"it takes a village to raise a child"* holds a great deal of wisdom.

My children have grown up living with their parents and grandparents since we bought our smallholding in 2003. Until relatively recently it's the way we would all have been raised, in a large family group. It's not been without challenges, but my three children have all benefitted from growing up in wonderful natural surroundings (pooling your money has definite advantages) and always having someone on hand to listen, help, or give them a lift to a friend's house! It has been a lifeline throughout my illness to have my mum and dad there for me, my husband and our children.

Try to embed whatever strategies you have to support your needs into your daily life, and make your work time and your free time part of the plan. Just as each need should be well supported, you should also aim for **each activity or element in your life to fulfil several needs**. Tree bark, for example, doesn't just do one job – it provides mechanical protection, regulates temperature, prevents moisture loss, protects from solar radiation, and changes its chemical composition to repel pests. Not bad for a gnarly piece of wood. Multi-functional bark means the tree uses its energy and resources effectively and is more resilient. By adopting the same approach we can be more efficient, feel less stressed (no more running around like a headless chicken), and it frees us up to meet more of the needs that are higher up Maslow's scale, like realising our full potential.

In fact you can make a single activity fulfil needs as diverse as health, belonging, creativity and self-confidence. For example, tending a vegetable plot means you can get fit, *and* de-stress, *and* eat healthy food, *and* be sociable (or be alone, whichever you need).

Analyse whether your activities are fulfilling more than one of your needs. Maybe your job is providing income but is also providing social contact *and* giving you a sense of fulfilment. If it doesn't, maybe it's time to create a livelihood that has wellbeing as a central pillar.

Notice that the hierarchy of needs doesn't include the need for 'stuff', such as all the latest technology, wardrobes full of clothes you'll seldom wear, and every type of kitchen gadget. If you need less stuff you can spend less time earning money and instead do more of what makes you come alive – experiences and activities. Mark Boyle, author of *The Moneyless Manifesto* shows how it is possible to live a fulfilled life without any money at all.[2]

Exercise

List each of your needs, then list three activities that can support each need. Your needs might include physical, financial, material, personal, emotional, psychological and others.

Feed your roots

"A tree with strong roots laughs at storms."

Malay proverb

There is a spruce tree in Sweden that has a small amount of top growth but has roots that have been dated at 9500 years old! As Peter Wohlleben states in *The Hidden Life of Trees*:

"The root is certainly a more decisive factor than what is growing above ground. After all, it is the root that looks after the survival of an organism."[1]

For us, having roots means feeling connected and grounded. Next time you go outside, stand barefoot and imagine yourself having roots pulling you down onto the earth. Your roots can be a physical location, cultural connections, family and friends, or a set of values that anchor you. Whatever they are, it's important to feed and nurture them. If your roots are strong you can survive some pruning of your top growth, or even a lightning strike, and re-grow stronger.

Strong roots anchor us, and allow us to 'dig deep' when times are tough. The long roots of jojoba trees in the Sonoran desert can draw water from 10 metres underground. The longest roots (those of a South African fig) are 120 metres long. However, our modern world offers our roots the equivalent of a shallow sprinkling of chemical fertiliser that is superficial and short-acting. These 'chemical fertilisers' include advertising, throwaway gadgets, fast food, social media, fast fashion and celebrity culture – very different from the deep and meaningful experiences we could be having. Interestingly, industrial agriculture treats plants' roots with the same superficial and damaging consideration that modern consumer economies treat us as individuals. Compare that to deep-rooted forests and lives full of purpose and meaning.

Root growth should continue throughout your life as times change. Coastal redwoods continue to build roots upwards (on top of their existing roots), as silt deposits are laid down. In doing so, they survive floods and develop incredibly strong root systems to hold up their trunks, the tallest of which reaches to 111 metres.

Your roots need to be strong enough to allow you to care for yourself, but also to care for other people, and to play your part in caring for all living things.

In addition to feeding your roots, remember to feed internal aspects of yourself as well, but **only feed what you want to grow**. If you sometimes feel a destructive, unhelpful 'voice' inside you, don't feed it. Crowd out its light and restrict its growth. Instead, feed the positive, loving, accepting and appreciating voice – heap compost on it, water it, and wait for it to blossom.

Exercise

What do you consider to be your roots, anchoring you? How can you support those roots and grow additional ones?

Waste nothing, recycle everything

"Though a tree grows so high, the falling leaves return to the roots."
Malay Proverb

There is no such thing as waste in the natural world. Remember our little beech nut and its 1.8 million siblings that didn't make it? None of them went to waste. They became food for birds and mice, then eventually returned to the earth where they could feed future generations of beech trees. We think of decay as bad, but without fungi and bacteria to break down matter we would be many metres deep in timber and dead animals rather than dark, rich life-sustaining soil. Think of decay as efficient recycling and you'll never look at a mouldy apple in the same way again.

The most stunning example of recycling in deciduous trees comes in autumn – those glorious yellow and orange colours are revealed when the green chlorophyll pigment breaks down and its constituent chemicals move back into the tree branches before the leaves fall, to be re-used in new growth next spring. These annual recycling events, which can be seen in the forests of New England, are even visible from space.

In a healthy system, every product that can't be recycled represents an energy leak, and we already know that nature doesn't like expending unnecessary energy. So any waste product from one living thing finds a new use by another. Even the oxygen we breathe originated as a waste product – of green bacteria. Imagine how different the evolution of life on Earth would have been without that feat of recycling.

For us, avoiding waste is not simply about recycling cans and bottles, re-using shopping bags, or limiting landfill – it's about our personal lives too. We can waste opportunities, and time that could be put to more effective or more pleasant use. Few of us will look back on our deathbeds and wish we had watched more cat videos, played more bobble games, or spent more time in shopping centres.

However, we do sometimes need to redefine waste. As Auguste Rodin said:

"Nothing is a waste of time if you use the experience wisely".

Often what we think of as 'wasted' time is actually rest, rejuvenation, a time to reflect on our lives, an opportunity for learning or to lay the foundations for a burst of creativity. If that's the case, then we would be wise to redefine it as productive, and stop putting it in the 'wasteful' (guilt-inducing) category.

What about relationships? Rates of relationship breakdown are sky high. That partly reflects the recognition that no-one should stay in a relationship that is damaging or violent. But it also perhaps demonstrates an unwillingness to stick at things when times get tough – perhaps because of illness (as in the case of myself and my husband), or having children, or periods of change like mid-life, or any number of other challenges that life throws at us. By staying together and actively working to improve communication, being open to our feelings, and seeking support, we can often transform our relationships for the better. They will then be based on the firm foundations of trust and mutual support. When my husband and I reflect on a particularly difficult time we experienced – dealing with my post-natal depression, three children under five, a new house and him working long hours in a new job – we agree that if we could get through that we can get through anything! I am so relieved we decided not to waste our experience and instead put the effort in to make things better.

In a natural system everything (and everyone) has value. We've all known someone who seems like they don't quite 'fit in', indeed many of us have had those feelings ourselves. Instead of seeing them as outsiders we could instead view them as we might look at trees growing in the wrong place (though maybe it's the 'judge' that's in the wrong place!). Many people call these plants weeds, but since I've been studying natural systems I have come to love weeds! Stinging nettles are considered weeds in the UK, but they are excellent sources of nitrogen to feed other plants. In fact it's believed that they were brought to Britain by the Romans as a mineral-rich food source. Instead of writing people off if they seem obnoxious or don't conform to 'the norm', we can try to identify each person's unique talents and nurture them, or help the person into a niche where they can thrive.

Natural systems are closed-loop systems, where nothing needs to be brought in and nothing is taken out. For example, trees obtain everything they need right where they are, and when they're no longer directly useful, their leaves and branches are turned back into food for themselves and other organisms. Try to create circular systems in your life. This might be buying local food, then composting any waste to feed your plants (wormeries can compost cooked and uncooked food and can be used indoors too). You could lobby manufacturers to only make goods that are 100% recyclable; or you might bring together your community to support local producers.

The thousands of square miles of plastic 'rafts' in the ocean are terrifying evidence that there is no such place as 'away', when we throw items in the trash. Ironically, the fact that we now eat fish that have consumed the plastic that we have thrown into our seas provides a terrifying example of nature's closed-loop systems.

Be creative in thinking how your 'waste problem' could be someone else's 'resource solution'. Using waste cooking oil to power cars, and used coffee grounds as a medium for growing mushrooms are two practical solutions. Similarly, your problem of boredom might be someone else's solution to needing company or wanting shelves put up. Your problem of paying for petrol may be another person's solution for getting to work; or your problem of having too much furniture might be someone else's solution to kitting out their first home.

But, above all, the best way to avoid waste to **take no more than you need**. Be minimalist – keep only items that are useful or beautiful. A tree doesn't take up all the water, leaving none for its competitors. And it doesn't pump out waste that can't be used by other organisms. We can't say the same about the carbon dioxide we are pumping into the atmosphere at a terrifying rate. As Henry David Thoreau said:

"Shall we always study to obtain more of these things and not sometimes be content with less?" [1]

In the case of forests, whose cover of the earth's surface is created by taking no more than they need, then less is definitely more.

Exercise

Examine the waste in your life. What are you wasting in terms of time, energy, emotions and opportunities? Can you reduce your consumption of material 'stuff' to a minimum?

Value local, biological and renewable resources

"The fairest thing in nature, a flower, still has its roots in earth and manure."

D.H. Lawrence

All life on Earth is made up of just a small number of elements – carbon, hydrogen, oxygen, nitrogen, phosphorus and sulphur (and a couple of handfuls of trace elements to add a spice mix to the curry of life). Many of the elements within us (and in trees) originated in stars, whose dust is scattered through the universe.

With those ingredients, life has created the most amazing feats of engineering: the strongest of materials (like spider silk and pearls); non-stop flight without refuelling (7000 miles/11,500 km from Alaska to New Zealand by the bar-tailed godwit); soil-erosion prevention (tree roots); water-repellent surfaces (leaves); solar generators (chlorophyll); super-efficient power stations (mitochondria); anti-bacterial products (bee propolis); dams that alter the course of vast rivers (beavers); rot-resistant building materials (the alder pillars used to create Venice); the creation of rain (forests); desalination (mangroves); the removal of heavy metals from soil (willow) and many, many more...

Nature does all this with no toxic waste that can't be recycled into some other life-form, and usually with resources found in a very small local area. As Isaac Newton said:

"Nature is pleased with simplicity and nature is no dummy".

I interpret this to mean that, while nature itself is diverse and complex, it uses simple methods to achieve greatness.

The most incredible thing about natural systems is that, as time passes, they increase in size and complexity. They are more than renewable (replacing resources), they are regenerative – they use and recycle resources in ways that result in more being available (often in different forms) to themselves and other living beings. An example is the way that forests create soil, providing

113

habitats and nutrients for billions of organisms, building layer upon layer each year. They don't erode, they create abundance.

By contrast, the human systems that have been established in the last 400 years (economic, social, financial, industrial and energy-related) have depleted the earth's resources and have ignored what we could learn from nature; that we could instead be contributing to the creation of new life and a gradual yet continual increase in 'wealth' for all. The irony is that we call our systems 'growth' but, by using up resources at staggering rates, with no mechanisms to renew or build on them, we diminish what we have, when we could be creating more prosperity upon prosperity.

What does the principle of 'local, biological and renewable' mean for us on a personal level? It means being 'productive' (creating things), 'efficient' (not wasteful), and only taking the means necessary to thrive (don't worry, nature's solutions offer us much more than mere survival). It means redefining 'outputs' and 'yields' and 'achievements' and 'success' in terms of non-financial gains like friendship, belonging, support, autonomy, self-esteem and fulfilment. It means acting like a contented great-great grandparent who lived modestly and didn't need pointless belongings (well maybe a porcelain dog on the mantelpiece, but we'll skip over that). They owned or borrowed items that could be used to create other things (like a sewing machine, tools, a trowel or a spade, or a set of paints and canvas). Our ancestors often had to turn their hand to many tasks, without feeling that they had to be experts. Learning from them, we can replace consumption with creativity, and in the process build self-esteem and self-reliance. Think of yourself as a renewable and regenerative resource creating more with what you already have.

Invest in the people in your life, by meeting up regularly, picking up the phone or talking on the internet. Their friendship and support will grow as you feed it. The 'renewable resources' in our community woodland project aren't just the straw bales and the timber used to construct our roundhouse, they are the volunteers who come back week after week to share in creating something from scratch – forests, education, community activities, friendships and collaborative relationships (even romance!).

Finally, if you would like to witness the superior value of renewable resources then take a young child for a walk in the outdoors and give them the choice of an expensive plastic toy or a stick. The plastic may be shiny and colourful, but it will soon be discarded in favour of the stick, which will be transformed into a magic wand, a fishing rod, a sword, a crown or a unicorn's horn. Stand back and watch the magic happen when you put that piece of tree in their hand.

Case study

One of my biggest personal lessons in using renewable resources came on the day of a big presentation, which I was giving in an outdoor venue. In front of an audience of around 40 people, the generator powering the projector broke. I was forced to ditch the photos and speak from my heart about the three years of design work that I had carried out. Afterwards, the audience said that there was no need for photos. I now teach all of my courses and workshops with a home-made wooden flip-chart, or a few pieces of paper, since I realised that nothing can beat renewable in terms of resilience, and nothing can beat speaking from a passionate standpoint, which is ultimately endlessly renewable.

Exercise

Which resources in your life could you switch from non-renewable to renewable? Think about material items, but also personal attributes and relationships.

Group 4 Principles

Connection

Know that everything is connected

"Everything is in some way connected to everything else."
Leonardo da Vinci

Plunge your hand into a forest floor and you'll find a white web of activity. Hidden beneath the soil is a network of mycorrhizal fungi connecting trees, communicating their needs and allowing them to share nutrients. This system allows established trees to give to others in need and thus maintain the health of the whole forest. Via this web, trees can even keep otherwise dead stumps alive by giving them food when the leafless stump can no longer photosynthesise.[1] There are 'hub' or 'parent' trees too – older trees that form key hubs central to the fungal communication system, and when these are removed by foresters unaware of their vital role, the health of the whole forest suffers. Of course the mycorrhizal fungi do not offer their communication service for free – they are paid in sugars from the trees' roots.

I discovered the hard way that a lack of these fungi slows growth, when we planted the young trees at Whistlewood. In my own woodland we had planted the saplings with roots soaked in mycorrhizal fungi, but neglected to do so for the community woodland trees. The difference in growth is remarkable. Those trees will eventually find and spread their own fungal networks, but that takes time. Planting my own woodland was like building a town with a ready-made, fully functioning internet system – while at Whistlewood it was more like allowing each home to be connected only once their neighbour had joined up.

Zoom out and you'll see that plant, animal and fungal networks exist everywhere, connecting each individual into interacting groups. Then these systems join with other ecosystems, on and on, until there is one giant dynamic mass that is planet Earth. Furthermore, when living beings connect – whether plants, fungi, animals or human animals – there are emergent properties that cannot be predicted. These are outcomes quite different from what you'd expect from simply adding the two effects. That's the great marvel of life. One of these magical connections happened when a single bacterium entered a primitive cell – the resulting symbiotic relationship eventually led to the evolution of mitochondria, the cell organelles that release energy from food molecules through respiration in all modern plants and animals. Who could have anticipated that this interaction would lead to a world of diversity, including worms, kestrels, ash trees, dahlias, sheep, grass, bees and people, all interacting with each other? And that's just a fraction of what you might see on a short walk in the English countryside.

For ourselves, connections hold the same strength. Brené Brown in her book *The Gifts of Imperfection* defines connection as:

"the energy that exists between people when they feel seen, heard and valued; when they can give and receive without judgment; and when they derive sustenance and strength from the relationship."[2]

We often feel most alive when we are connecting with people – our bodies give us hits of oxytocin and cortisol, our neurons fire, and we have a glow of excitement and empathy. We may have never even met the person before the spark happens. We can also form emotional relationships with animals – millions of us have pets because of the unique relationships they offer. Connection can happen in unexpected ways – many a recreational hunter has looked into the eyes of their prey and decided they no longer wish to kill for sport. But it's not only animals that we can create bonds with – if we gave ourselves permission, we could 'meet' our own relatives in the tree world too and feel similar emotions. When we make the effort to connect with all living beings, rather than seeing ourselves as separate, it feels both comforting and exciting to discover a sense of belonging not only as part of human societies, but among the plant and animal world too.

In science, it is often individual elements that are studied – whether in plants, animals or people – without looking at the connections between them. When we look at any two individuals we should really be seeing three things – individual one, individual two, and the connection between them. That connection has a 'life' of its own – just as when you bring two quite different friends together at a party, say, and find they both play musical instruments. Before you know it you've accidentally created the next up-and-coming rock band!

119

Acting as a connector, like those magical fungi, is one of the most important roles you can play. The two people you are joining together will gain, since the more connections we all make, the more creativity and dynamic interactions can occur. And you will also benefit, by acting as a 'hub' tree *and* as someone who is joined to the network. Nature grows not with individuals, but with interactions between individuals, groups and ecosystems.

When we all sit at home in our isolated worlds, we break those bonds and struggle to make new ones. In many households, family members, all with their separate gadgets, sit on their own and may seldom come together. Our modern lives draw us apart, often through no fault of our own. A regular family meal, sat round a table on as many nights as possible, can be an opportunity for children of all ages to learn how to communicate effectively, and to learn to cook, practise sharing skills, and de-stress from their busy days. Parents become role models for healthy eating (and healthy communication too) and fussiness is not so much of an option when everyone is eating the same meal. As the children get older they can take on their share of cooking. (Although, when that happened in our household, my son's delicious meals risked bankrupting us, as they involved the most expensive and obscure ingredients, available only on the internet or at specialist shops! But of course I'm not complaining about living with someone who enjoys good food.)

I believe we create stronger family bonds when everyone takes their share of the cooking and the chores. Equal gender roles are particularly important, with dads and boys carrying out similar tasks as mums and girls (and vice versa). There has been some concern that moves towards growing food and cooking from scratch have the potential to exacerbate gender divides, and that is certainly something we should watch out for. The last thing we want is to return to the gender stereotypes of the 1950s! As with everything in our modern world, finding the balance can be tricky – you'll need to make an active decision about how best to work it within your own circumstances.

Making time to connect as a family can also lead to new experiences and unexpected benefits. There are many family events and festivals to explore. My favourite is the Timber

Festival[3] in the National Forest near to where I live – a weekend of storytelling, music, discussions, performances, spectacles, and local food and ale, all in a beautiful relaxed woodland setting. One of the most exciting elements is that the organisers make it their mission to bring people together as collaborators in the event, rather than merely consumers. The activities stimulate discussion, facilitate connection, and bring strangers together to explore the magic of trees, woodlands and all that they offer.

It may seem counter to everything we normally tell our kids, but talking to strangers (with parents and with appropriate guidance) has great benefits for children, and is something that increases awareness of the world, and encourages empathy and appreciation of diversity. In the past we have welcomed voluntary workers who stay to work and learn about smallholding, in exchange for a room and food.[4] Our children gained from meeting new people and seeing new perspectives on life. This wasn't always easy – in fact, one guy really outstayed his welcome, but we have a fantastically productive orchard now that we planted with him, along with the sense of achievement that our young children felt at having taught him how to use a hand screwdriver for the first time. And they gained an insight into the life of someone who did not have a secure home, as they have been fortunate to have.

One thing we can observe about natural connections is that they **work both ways**. This encourages us to see things from the other person's (or other living being's) perspective. If I am hurting you, you are being hurt. If you are taking me out to dinner, I am being taken out to dinner; if you chop down a tree, the tree is being chopped down. Often the language we use reverses when we are taking 'negative' action versus 'positive' action, to try and avoid the emotional side-effects. It's a lot easier to say *"I can see you are hurt"* rather than *"I can see that I have hurt you"*. We are much more likely to take ownership of a pleasant action – *"I gave her a present"* rather than *"she received a present"* Taking responsibility for any hurt is important in order to strengthen relationships. This means accepting that we are human, and that we make mistakes, while avoiding the self-shame that tells us we are a 'bad person' for accidentally hurting or offending someone. Sometimes a heartfelt apology is enough, and the mycorrhizal network of positive energy between you can start flowing again. Other times you may have to work harder to rebuild a relationship, while keeping the channels of communication open.

When we meet someone new (or bring different people together) everyone benefits if we can find common ground – finding the characteristics we share rather than those that separate us. Occasionally, the most fervent racist has met with a person from a different culture and discovered the things they have in common, establishing a friendship based on mutual connection. That starts when one person reaches out with compassion, with an open mind and a willingness to understand.

Working from the opposite direction, if someone has hurt you it's important to let them know, rather than letting resentments fester. But be gentle and compassionate – they may not be as open to feedback as you might hope (they may not have yet encountered the wisdom and value of self-regulation and feedback contained in the natural world!).

By observing nature we can often see that what is 'good for you' is also 'good for me' – so if we meet and I offer to cook you a meal, I too can enjoy the meal and the company as well. On a societal level, when we care for the most vulnerable we all gain by lower crime rates, lower healthcare costs, and better community cohesion, in addition to it simply being the right thing to do.

Try to make positive connections wherever you go – since everything is connected, you are going to have an impact, so make it a positive one. You won't just affect one person – you'll be spreading positivity further throughout the network, leading to benefits you will never know about. If you chase after someone at the checkout because they've left their debit card in the card reader (yes this has happened to me), you may prevent the busy parent from having to return to the supermarket, their child then missing their football match, and a whole family spending their evening stressed. But you may never know that, and that's OK.

Smiles are infectious too. In our town many people say hello to each other and smile when they walk down the street. We often say thank you when we are driving and someone else lets us pass. But when we lived in London my smiles were mainly met with suspicion – I was that crazy woman grinning on the daily commute! That doesn't mean that people in London are less friendly, but we become culturally conditioned to follow others, particularly their facial expressions. It sometimes takes courage to be the only one smiling, but if you make the effort there will be at least one person in your day who will pass that smile on.

By contrast, when we encounter violent, hurtful or traumatic experiences at the hands of someone else, or read the news full of murder and conflict, it's hard to resist the feeling that people in general are horrible, or against you. But look closer and you can see that there are folk all over the world caring for others, making meals for their neighbours, helping strangers after car crashes, risking their lives to rescue animals, protesting at injustice, and travelling to help in disaster zones. It's just that we see these things less frequently in the news. Whether your contribution tomorrow is big or small, take the courage to look for the best in the people you meet and you will start to have your faith in human nature restored.

I believe that we should strongly resist the point of view that we've been sold in the Western world since the 1980s that depending on or supporting others (either as individuals or with infrastructure like a welfare state, free healthcare system or pensions) is a sign of weakness. We can be strong individuals *and* be part of a mighty forest. If governments, corporations and other organisations acted more like woodland ecosystems with parent oak trees redistributing nutrients in beneficial ways, the health of the whole would improve drastically. Remember also that forests don't conform to national boundaries – countries are something invented in the minds of people (largely in the minds of just a few colonialists). The message from our tree cousins is to share with others around the world, break down national and regional boundaries, preserve identity, but increase connectivity.

Just as trees move from less hospitable areas of the planet to more fertile ones as circumstances change (such as pioneer species did after the retreat of the last Ice Age), then we should not think it unreasonable for people to do the same when their surroundings become intolerable, such as during wars or when they experience persecution. Refugees may be forced by circumstances to move, just as trees can be – but they then become contributors in their new location.

Finally, I want to tell you about walnut trees. They are relatively unusual in that they give out chemicals from their roots to repel other trees (the old wisdom is never to plant an apple near a walnut). In my opinion we should make sure that we are voting the oak trees – the strong connectors of the political world – into office, not the walnuts that want to repel alien species. (Please, walnut lovers, don't write in – though I can see why you might be annoyed at having your favourite tree compared to some of the current world leaders.)

Wherever you live, go out there, be brave, make connections, repair the broken ones, then thank the trees for leading the way.

Case study

I love the way that AJ describes his connection with the living world. Even just reading his words I feel calmer.

"My knowledge that my thought patterns are impacted by my experience of living in a city where the density of population continues to grow and the amount of activity and sensory and stimulation around me is more than I can process. Every day I go to the river, or a pond, or lake or the sea if I am away from home. I take time to sit and be there, noticing what is going on inside me and outside of me. I spend 20 minutes there, following whatever impulse I feel once I am there, sitting, standing, dancing with the feeling of the place and time, collecting sometimes seeds, flowers, leaves, feathers, or dangling my legs in the water, might be walking, I never know, just let this emerge, the intention is connection, to make contact with myself and let in the world.

One day I was looking at the beech trees by the river, looking at the bark, it was early autumn, I think. I was marvelling at the surface of the bark, and feeling as if a body, a limb, like my arm, feeling the circulation within the tree, the movement of water, the changing pressure with gravity, standing and leaning, moving to sense the changing flow in the bark, and it was as if the tree became alive, a strange feeling, moving in front of my eyes. That morning I stayed over an hour on the river bank, losing track of the time yet in some ways gaining a greater sense awareness of time, the seasons and the ecology of the river bank. My whole day was flowing and I felt a great sense of stillness as if the being of the tree were inside me and I was noticing all the detail of life around me outside of my skin."

How many different connections do you have in your life? Write them round the edge of a circle. Draw lines between all the elements. A healthy and resilient system is one that has many diverse connections.

Value diversity

"To such an extent does nature delight and abound in variety that among her trees there is not one plant to be found which is exactly like another; and not only among the plants, but among the boughs, the leaves and the fruits, you will not find one which is exactly similar to another."

Leonardo da Vinci

It's remarkable that we can see back in time to the Big Bang, we know about quarks, black holes and the Higgs boson, but we have no idea how many species are here on our home planet. Estimates are somewhere between two million and one trillion[1] – that's an enormous margin of error! Scientists can't even agree on what constitutes a species. It's generally recognised that species are different when they can't breed fertile offspring, but even then there are exceptions. When it comes to trees, estimates are somewhere over 60,000 different species.[2] And remember, not only is each species different, but every single individual within a species is unique too.

Diversity creates strength, adaptability and resilience, and allows for creative new strategies – better ways of responding to changing circumstances. Trees have amazing methods for ensuring this diversity is maintained in their offspring. For example, the bird cherry invented genetic testing long before humans did – their flowers test incoming pollen and close the tube leading to the ovary if the pollen matches their own, thus avoiding self-pollination, which would result in less genetic variation in the offspring. Avocado plants prevent self-pollination by opening their flowers twice, with all the flowers on each plant opening at the same time to expose first the female and then subsequently the male parts.

The offspring of genetically quite different parents can often be stronger or fitter in some way than either of the parent organisms, as their genetic contributions are mixed together. This is called 'hybrid vigour'. For example, the small-leaved lime and the large-leaved lime formed a natural hybrid – the healthy and strong common lime. By contrast, a lack of diversity in a population creates weakness, as we saw with Dutch elm disease, which wiped out almost all of the elms in the UK in the 1970s. All the elms were genetically very similar, and when the elm bark beetle arrived from Asia very few could defend themselves. Luckily nurseries are now able to breed resistant varieties from those elms whose genetic differences allowed them to survive.

As humans, we also have hybrid vigour, thanks to countless generations of unions between genetically dissimilar people. (I discovered when I carried out a genetic test that I have a small percentage of Neanderthal in me! It's not just me – most people of non-African genetic heritage have the same 'Neanderthal genes'.) On the other hand, marriages between close European royal family members, who were obviously genetically very similar, meant that genes for illnesses such as haemophilia, of which Queen Victoria was a carrier, were more likely to be expressed. Sixteen of Victoria's descendants had haemophilia.

So, how can we harness the benefits that diversity brings? We can learn to value the different perspectives, experiences and knowledge that we all bring to the world. Our different cultures might be expressed through art, music, philosophy, clothing or cuisine, for example. Fusion cuisine brings together dishes from different cultures, and creates exciting new flavours and experiences. One of Britain's favourite dishes is chicken tikka masala – a blend of Anglo-Indian influences.

Lack of discrimination is the cornerstone of the protection of diversity, but valuing difference goes far beyond non-discrimination. Anti-discrimination laws are vital, but they put the accent on things we shouldn't do, rather than stressing that having a diversity of people and of views is positively beneficial. Forests encourage us to change our mindsets and see communities that are different, not as a threat, but as a positive benefit, bringing in fresh ideas and unique talents. This includes refugees and migrants, any person of a different race, religion, culture, gender, sexuality or disability. For example, many extraordinarily talented people in the modern era have been refugees – such as Freddie Mercury, Gloria Estefan, Sigmund Freud, Isabel Allende, Albert Einstein and Madeleine Albright.

If you are an employer, look at whether your hiring practices can harness the different skills that people with disabilities or non-neurotypical ways of thinking offer, like people on the autism spectrum or with dyslexia. Silicon Valley companies are now realising that different ways of thinking can add benefits in terms of problem-solving, innovation and creativity.

In business, performance conversations based on strengths can be more effective than those that try and address perceived weaknesses. In a woodland, if all trees were judged against the yardstick of who grew straightest and quickest we would give alders first prize. We might reward them with extra nutrients (in human terms this might be additional praise, or a payrise) and delay the growth of oaks and beeches with their slower development and less uniform habits (by frequently asking their human equivalents why they are not achieving the results expected).

Let's value people with non-academic talents too. Our education system here in the UK is progressively narrowing the range of subjects offered, to the detriment of practical, creative and artistic skills. Education systems that focus too much on testing (of children and teachers) risk marginalising children whose talents lie outside of this narrow band. But there are alternatives. In 2016, Finland (which rates consistently highly in the UN's Education Index) introduced learning based on the study of topics and themes in a holistic way, and restructured the education system for 7–16-year-olds to focus on collaboration, creativity, communication and critical thinking.

If workplaces and education systems were organised according to the principles of the forest, we could see how each person has different needs and can contribute in a variety of distinct and important ways. Some are fast-growing pioneers while others develop more slowly; some are bold and showy while others prefer the shade; and some need sheltering more than others. There are those that find their place later, in niches created by the early adopters, and some hide their contribution underground. It helps to have some mycorrhizal fungi, facilitating communication. It's the duty of all members to add rich organic matter to feed the group. And it goes without saying that every single individual contributes to the whole and should be valued for their contribution.

Finally, it's important to recognise that what we have in common is always more important than that which separates us.[3] We are all human beings; we all share the same emotions, fears and joy. We all mourn when we lose someone, we all empathise when someone else is in pain and we all celebrate when something amazing happens. Let's celebrate what unites us and value the ways we are different.

Exercise

Does your workplace or organisation encourage diversity? How could you help create that hybrid vigour of ideas, talents and personalities?

Cultivate co-operative relationships

*"Evolution did not intend trees to grow singly. Far more than ourselves
they are social creatures, and no more natural as isolated specimens
than man is as a marooned sailor or hermit."*

John Fowles

When we think about evolution, what often springs to mind is
the *'survival of the fittest'* – which suggests a mass of violent beings
all fighting each other for life. However, Darwin's view of the
natural world equally involved *"dependence of one being on another"*.
Similarly, evolutionary biologist Richard Dawkins, author of *The
Selfish Gene*,[1] has stated that his book could equally have been
called *The Co-operative Gene* without changing a single word of the
text. He explains that *"Selfishness and co-operation are two sides of a
Darwinian coin"*.[2] Genes are indeed 'selfish', operating in ways that
ensure their DNA is carried forward, but this often happens
through co-operation between organisms – through connections
between living things that promote the individual's overall aims.

At a basic level cells co-operate, and this involves self-
sacrifice. Our own bodies have 10 trillion cells all working
together. Sadly, up to half of us in the UK will experience first-
hand what happens when that collaboration goes wrong.[3] When
the normal cell-signalling mechanisms break down, cancer cells
multiply uncontrollably, destroy healthy cells and, if not treated,
may eventually kill the host organism, and kill themselves in the
process. It's a tragic reminder of the importance of working
together.

Often co-operative relationships involve some kind of
direct mutual benefit, such as when aphids in a tree canopy offer
honeydew, and ants offer protection to those aphids in return.
Horse chestnut trees help their pollinating bees conserve energy
by changing the colour of their flowers from yellow to orange
once a bee has successfully visited, thus ensuring more of their
own flowers are pollinated. Bacteria on the roots of peas and
beans gain sugars, while offering nitrogen to the host plant.

As species co-evolve, they build up more and more
beneficial connections – the British native pedunculate oak
supports over 400 species of life, but the imported holm oak is

home to very few. The more connections there are, the healthier and more resilient the ecosystem.

Nature **aggregates scattered elements into something greater** – the effect is regenerative and creative rather than merely 'sustainable'. We can see this in action when cells work together in trees, and trees together create climate-stabilising forests.

For trees, and for ourselves, collaboration creates efficiency. By sharing knowledge and resources, we produce less waste, can create collective intelligence, and have no need to constantly 'reinvent the wheel'.

Competition, of course, can have benefits – let's not underestimate the progress that can be made when two organisms strive for similar goals. But in nature as well as in business, competition has the potential to create inefficiencies. When medical research, for example, is based solely on competition, researchers are denied access to information that could shortcut the process of developing treatments. Often non-profitable solutions, such as those based on freely available herbs, aren't taken forward. However, there are alternative ways of working. Open-source solutions in diverse fields (such as software, science, agriculture, architecture, film-making and education) harness collective wisdom, and each contributor offers their time and knowledge for the good of the whole, often for free. This is very different from the economic theories that state that competition is the sole motivator and that people only do things that they perceive to be maximising their own short-term self-interest.

In the workplace, models such as systems thinking (modelled on natural systems), holocracy (an organisational system characterised by self-organising teams with decentralised decision-making and authority), and consensus decision-making, put in place more effective ways of managing both for-profit and not-for-profit organisations. Innovative systems of communication and knowledge-sharing create safe spaces for each person to speak, which help retain staff and promote innovation and progress. This makes for a more pleasant working environment and efficiency gains too – win–wins.

The internet offers many examples of individuals coming together to create something new, such as crowd-funding,

Wikipedia, Airbnb, microfinance, online dating (when done well), health support forums, and platforms sharing creative solutions to climate change. All these platforms facilitate communication, and benefit millions as a result.

Some relationships have elements of both competition and co-operation. In Hay-on-Wye, a small town in Wales, there are over 20 bookshops competing for business. However, the bookshops attract literature lovers from around the world and that creates larger markets for everyone. The bookshop cluster would never have developed if the first bookshop owner had been overly competitive and run the second out of town. In all areas of industry, guilds and business associations can bring entrepreneurs together. On a small scale at Whistlewood we hold gatherings to facilitate collaborative endeavours, such as complementary therapists creating a hub for their services, rather than fearing each other as competitors.

It can often take a mind-shift to turn suspicion of the competition into opportunities to maximise benefits for both parties – we might be naturally wary that the other party might reject our advances and even take advantage of the situation. However, the risk is worth the potential rewards and as time goes on the culture can gradually shift when others realise the benefits for profits as well as for people.

It may come as a surprise to discover that there are few hierarchical organisational structures in the 'super-organisms' that we find in nature. (Super-organisms are large numbers of a particular species all working together in a collaborative way for a common goal, examples of which are bees, ants, orcas, elephants and crows). In a hive there are no managers or bosses. A queen bee doesn't tell the workers what to do – each bee has its own role and will work to maximise the health and success of the whole colony. Bees perform their 'waggle dances' – figures of eight pointing to the direction of new nectar supplies or potential nest sites. Ants, with no need for 'fat-cat' bosses, come together in clusters, communicating to show others where the best food is.[4]

Instead of a hierarchical business, why not create or join a co-operative society, where all members and customers benefit, rather than a few bosses and shareholders? Co-operatives and not-for-profit organisations have wider goals than purely financial profitability. They often measure yields in a variety of ways, including ethical considerations, which in turn influences the behaviour of managers and employees.

In our personal lives we can seek mutual co-operation too. To do so we must build trust, and we only achieve that by taking the risk that someone else may harm something we value. We cannot create such magical life experiences as falling in love, having children and making new friends if we don't put ourselves out there with the realisation that we might get hurt.

And finally, co-operation often breeds co-operation (such as when ants form lines to transport food, stray ants join in, often adding their own knowledge of the best food source) – we can observe another of those virtuous spirals that we see again and again in nature, creating fertile ground for sustainable and regenerative growth.

Exercise

Take a look at all the relationships (personal and professional) that you have in your life. Are they built on co-operation? How equal and mutually beneficial are they? What could you do to promote collaboration?

Integrate don't segregate

"Ecologically speaking, the music of the spheres is neither a solo
nor a massed chorus carrying a single melody
but a jazz improvisation where each player has a riff."

Theodore Roszak[1]

If forests were on the same trajectory as our human societies, they might look something like this: the trees would decide that all the saplings would be raised separately and the older trees uprooted and put in their own plantation. An oak might think that some bees were freeloaders, taking too much nectar in return for pollination, so they would no longer merit the shelter of a branch. Woodpeckers would definitely be cast out – like naughty teenagers making too much noise. Bats might be criticised for keeping anti-social hours. Trees that didn't engage in heterosexual reproduction would probably have difficulties. Females might be paid less in nutrients than their male counterparts, and males might be overly categorised as aggressive. Each tree or species would tend to distrust the others, sometimes descending into all-out war. Of course that is a broad generalisation, both of the woodland and of our societies, but it's striking how different our modern world is to the integrated, dynamic harmony of the forest.

The effect of evolution, since its earliest days, has been for species to evolve in response to each other's presence in their ecosystem. They create bonds as they do so, whether it be through feeding relationships, competitive relationships, by providing protection or a place to live. As more and more relationships are formed, the individual become part of an increasingly complex ecosystem – they are not separated from it, but are integrated into the whole. If the most effective method of survival for the past 3.8 billion years was for individuals to isolate themselves, then that's what we would see now rather than a wonderful mass of interconnected beings.

So how can we learn from the inter-dependence of organisms in ecosystems? Start by integrating the people closest to you. That might mean introducing your friends to your family, or connecting colleagues. You can make efforts to integrate yourself into your community by joining a local organisation or participating in a leisure activity nearby, rather than jumping in the car and heading out of town. You may be able to integrate your work with your local community if you look for a job close to home or set up a business selling to a market nearby.

Towns and villages can hold gatherings to help with this process. In the UK, many villages have their own festivals where people come together to celebrate – some are stranger than others. In Gloucester, the townspeople gather each year to roll giant wheels of cheese down a steep hill at speeds of up to 90 miles per hour! Wassailing is my favourite – a celebration around Twelfth Night, shortly after the New Year, when people come together to thank fruit trees by playing music, putting toast in their branches, and pouring cider on their roots. It sounds strange but it's great fun and has historical significance in honouring and protecting the trees. It's also a good excuse to drink a large quantity of last year's cider harvest!

It's exciting when different cultures come together. Festivals such as the Notting Hill Carnival in London, and Diwali (the Hindu festival of light celebrated in style in my local town of Leicester) bring together diverse communities. In housing, we should be encouraging integration in communities, rather than creating ghettos and gated housing estates that divide people from different backgrounds. Sadly house price increases and property speculation are creating areas (for example, in London) where only the rich can afford to live. But there are alternatives created by affordable housing policies and regulation of landlords, rents and policies on second homes.

Community allotments can be great places to meet new people and to find out how to grow a host of exotic vegetables from the diverse cultures of different allotmenteers. And if you bring your children to learn from experienced older growers, you may witness the magic as they see their first lettuce seed start to sprout.

Mixing up the ages creates healthy communities – there is a nursery in London that has a pre-school in a residential home for older people[2]; and a housing association in the Netherlands that combines student housing with accommodation for people living with dementia.[3] Both ages benefit. Members of the older generation share their knowledge, and escape the isolation and loneliness that studies have shown shorten life expectancy as

135

much as obesity.[4] Isolated trees have shorter lives than those connected in forests, and the same is true of isolated people.[5]

Intentional communities, such as LILAC (Low Impact Living Affordable Community) in Leeds, UK (an eco-housing co-operative), combine people's needs for private living space with shared facilities, such as a 'common house' for shared meals, office space, meetings and play, and shared outdoor space – allotments, children's play area and pond.[6] Communities like these, in countries around the world, have long gone beyond the 'hippy' or 'alternative' label (not that I have anything against anyone who wants to identify as a hippy).

Finally, don't forget to integrate nature into your life and the life of others too. Bring the outdoors indoors, create gardens wherever you spend your time. Better still, get an allotment and integrate nature and people into your world.

Exercise

What can you do to bring together the different elements of your life?

Pick your battles

"But man is part of nature, and his war against nature
is inevitably a war against himself."

Rachel Carson[1]

Here's where we tackle the subject of competing interests, survival and the seemingly all-out war that rages in the natural world. This isn't some utopian book suggesting we can create a world without conflict, or pretending that nature always lives in harmony. We only have to head to the local park to see examples of trees jostling for space, water and light. Every individual of every species tries its hardest to survive.

However, we can observe that an organism that takes too much destroys its means of survival, which inevitably leads to its own death. We know this runs counter to its evolutionary aim. An example is the Spanish flu virus in the early twentieth century that killed 3–5% of the world's population. Had the virus continued on this trajectory, it would have eventually exhausted the number of hosts on which it relied; but it mutated to be less deadly and therefore has continued its life over millions more generations. In the animal world, lions choose the weakest prey from a herd and, when their bellies are full, they will allow a buffalo to saunter past unharmed.

Each species has ways, either direct or indirect, to ensure that it doesn't over-consume. In the tree world, honey fungus is a good example. Any gardener with the misfortune to come across it knows that it will kill mature trees in a matter of a few years. However, this great fungus has a monitoring system and chooses only weaker specimens and thus (in its natural habitat) benefits the forest as a whole, by creating space for new life. And, by not taking more than it needs, the fungus leaves itself future food sources.

Conflict is dangerous and energy-intensive, and is carried out only when it has a vital purpose for survival, rather than at random. It is true that there are numerous rampant, destructive species that wipe out others, but they are often non-native species. In the UK, Japanese knotweed and rhododendron are crowding out British native wildflowers, but they were imported by pioneering plant-hunters into environments that don't have

137

the mechanisms to keep them in check. If you keep chickens, you may despair at the devastation wreaked by foxes, but foxes and chickens would have never come into contact without humans – the original chickens being tree-roosting junglefowl from Asia.

Contrast these battles in the living world with the numerous conflicts that modern humans engage in for means other than survival. Both civil conflicts and wars between nation states (fought over artificially constructed boundaries totally meaningless to natural systems) often result in whole-system collapse, such as we are witnessing in Syria and Yemen. And while trees will do their utmost to get sufficient light, they don't have to be the biggest or tallest in their forest, like some people's egos propel them to be – in fact, those trees that tower too far above others are likely to get their crowns chopped off by strong winds (something Louis XVI would have been wise to think about prior to the French Revolution!).

On a personal level, our 'battles' are hopefully much smaller and less violent than all-out wars, but they have enormous impacts on our lives nonetheless. We can choose which battles are worth fighting, and seek out productive ways of resolving conflict rather than risk resorting to violence. Defending our rights and values may be as important as defending basic needs. I was immensely proud of my mother (who hates confrontation) when she tackled someone she met on holiday who assumed she was racist just because of her age. Go Mum!

So how can you avoid escalating a situation if someone is engaging in behaviour you don't find acceptable? Take a step back. Assess whether there are other factors influencing your emotions or their behaviour, such as alcohol, stress, drugs or a previous experience. Tiredness and illness can be factors too. I know I have a much shorter fuse when I am exhausted. You can agree to disagree, but it's important to gain some mutual understanding of the other person's point of view before you both let it rest. Ask them to explain what they feel without interruption and then reflect back what you understood. Agree a strategy for the other person to do the same for you.

When conflict does arise, there are techniques for restoring peace, such as saying sorry, owning your own emotions, listening and forgiveness. It may need a third party to facilitate, such as a friend, relationship counsellor or a skilled group facilitator. One useful mindset is to assume that the other person is doing the best they can at the time. You'll feel better through this way of perceiving others, since you will be released from the corresponding negative emotions, like defensiveness, self-doubt and taking things too personally.

One of the most important spheres in which to pick your battles is with children. If you have a toddler or a teenager, every encounter has the potential to escalate. Sometimes you may have to stand your ground (for example, when insisting your child wears a seatbelt), and other times it may be better to let it go (for instance, prising your teenager out of bed before noon at the weekend). Give them firm boundaries, and have appropriate and relevant consequences if they overstep them, but don't tie them (or you) to standards that are impossible to stick to. You will both be miserable and they risk becoming resentful and confused. Don't be a pushover – it's unhealthy for children to get everything they want. Aim for a dynamic equilibrium with long periods of relative calm and short periods of antagonism. They do need something to push against to be able to come out of the shadow of their parent tree.

In my experience, parenthood is a series of phases where you always feel slightly behind and are playing catch-up. Have confidence in your abilities and a willingness to learn how to be a better parent, and realise that the difficult time you are experiencing will not last. Aim to be a **good enough** parent, because there is no such thing as a perfect one.

Finally, a battle that is definitely not worth fighting is one that you have with yourself. Find strategies to silence those two competing gremlins that sit on opposite shoulders, pulling you in conflicting directions. Most of us have a critical, blaming voice that sits in judgement, holding us back and making us miserable. I lived with this voice for a long time and, after several long years of trying, finally learned to silence it (or at the very least to tell it to go away when it rears its ugly head from time to time). Try techniques such as mindfulness, meditation, CBT (cognitive behavioural therapy) or talking to supportive friends (my preferred method), to free your mind up for more beneficial thoughts and activities.

Exercise

Take time to walk in the forest and observe the ways in which trees and other plants and animals engage in battles. Notice how they are part of a dynamic whole, with no creature fighting more than is necessary.

Which battles in your life are worth fighting? What strategies do you have in place to resolve potential conflict without violence?

Accept feedback

*"In nature there are neither rewards nor punishments,
there are consequences."*

Robert Green Ingersoll

When exploring the principles in Group 2, we looked at self-regulation, and discovered the mechanisms that bring nature back into equilibrium, or amplify a particular action. We saw how that principle can be used to bring your own life back into balance. In this section we will explore feedback from a different perspective – giving and receiving 'feedback' from other people.

Earlier in the book we established that feedback is a good thing and that you can always find useful information contained within the message, even if you have to dig deep to find it. A system that avoids feedback eventually fails. It's the equivalent of closing your eyes and putting your fingers in your ears and then hoping that the tree falling your way won't hit you.

I have personally found that by looking at feedback in this positive and productive way (i.e. the way that trees do), I can seek opinions and responses from other people more openly, without as many of the consequent negative emotions. Of course it's still scary, but it honestly does work.

Feedback comes in several stages so let's explore them in relation to our own experiences. First there is the input of information. At this stage we have to recognise that we are not receiving perfect information. The other person may be talking, but are we listening? Sometimes there is too much happening at once so we can't possibly process it all. There are three filters we all tend to use when dealing with a mass of incoming information. First, we block out or delete a lot of what comes our way. The problem is that we may be losing the good bits and keeping the bad (often depending on the mood we are in). An example would be when we receive feedback from our boss, taking in the criticism and not hearing the praise (or vice versa). Second, we distort the information – we hear the information differently because of the person offering it, or the context. So you might be more open to advice from a friend you trust than from someone you don't know, even if the advice is the same. Third, we generalise what we hear from other scenarios – so if

141

someone has cheated on their partner in the past you might also assume that you can't trust them to give you feedback about bringing up your kids, even if they have never shown any hint of bad parenting. Once we recognise these three filters we can make a conscious decision to trust what we are hearing, or not, in full awareness of the context.

The next stage of feedback is to process the information. We do this on several different levels. Often the first reaction will be an unconscious one. When our boss calls us in for an appraisal and suggests ways we could improve, our heart rate may go up and our palms start to sweat, even if we agree with what they are saying. At this stage it's important to realise that your processing plant might be a little defective – if you're tired, hungry or unwell, anxiety increases. Anyone who suffers with migraines, immune-system diseases, mental health or anxiety-related issues, or a host of other illnesses, will know that stressful experiences don't have to be conscious ones, and they can trigger quite extreme reactions, sometimes in the presence of, or aimed towards, other people. The main point here is not to use these factors as an excuse for behaving badly, but if your physical reactions do impact on others you can be open about what's happening and the other person will hopefully realise that you're not trying to be difficult or hurtful. Of course, if you can try and use your conscious brain to calm the physical reactions down in the moment, then do so – breathing is the most important helper, or you may need to temporarily remove yourself from a situation.

Separate, but related to those physical symptoms, are emotional reactions. Emotions are good things – remember we said that they contain valuable information. Don't block them out, or you'll be storing up a whole lot of trouble for the future that may resurface as depression and anxiety, often decades later.

Try to work out the actual reason for your emotions. I will confess that I can over-react when I feel attacked, which I attribute to subconsciously not wanting to be the passive child who absorbed bullying for many years. It's something that I'm actively working on, now that I've put my finger on it as a root cause.

You may also be able to identify cultural factors that affect your ability to express your emotions in the ways you might wish, so if you are male, please ignore anyone who tells you to '*man up*' or that '*boys don't cry*'. If you're a woman don't listen to anyone who says '*you're being hysterical*' or tells you to '*calm down*'.

Then we get to the conscious brain processing bit. Having analysed all your previous emotional and physical reactions, you can put them to one side while you take in the actual message. The next phase in the feedback process is to decide what to do with the information. Remember it's a call to action. You could decide to ignore it (that's an action too) – you've considered it but you don't think the message is helpful to you. For example, if you are an activist or campaigner, you might choose not to take advice from someone without active experience in your field. Free speech is important, but that doesn't stop you concluding that many of the views expressed on the internet lack foundation. In even the most constructive online groups you may get only 1 in 100 comments worth taking seriously. If you take notice of abusive or groundless commentary, it will become pollution and you'll risk being poisoned by it. This is also one of those 'pick your battles' scenarios that we discussed in the previous principle.

Alternatively, what you could do is decide that there's something of use in the information that is coming in, and then consider what to do with it.

With practice you can go through this entire process quite quickly and that will free up your time for the most important stage of the feedback process – action! **Don't make the decision-making paralysing – nature likes productive**. Our oak tree that's being eaten by insects won't last long if it dithers over putting the tannins in its leaves.

The most empowering way of using the feedback process is to actively seek feedback in a constructive way and in a format that you can use. It takes courage, but it puts you in the driving seat. I often think of trees' roots actively seeking out useful information, and by thinking that way I can see the benefits of asking for feedback, rather than being paralysed by the fear of being caught off-guard by comments that come out of the blue. The feedback forms I give out after my courses ask participants what they have liked and what could be done differently. This format makes it much easier for me to act on their comments, adapting future courses based on their input.

Make sure you accept positive feedback too – often in the UK we are terrible at that. If you can't accept compliments from people, they'll feel awkward and will be less inclined to give them again. In our culture we are so unused to giving praise that it's often met with discomfort or cynicism, but don't let that put you off! Show your appreciation and recognise others' achievements. This is another of those positive spirals that has to have some energy input to start its upward trajectory.

If you are giving feedback, find the most constructive way to communicate it. Think how the other person will best be able to process it. Giving feedback is about guiding, increasing learning, and building confidence in the other person.

Above all, know that by remembering the way that trees use feedback, you can take control – you'll learn and grow, and become more resilient and productive.

Let's end with Aristotle:

"To avoid criticism say nothing, do nothing, be nothing".

To achieve your full potential you're going to have to be courageous and let yourself be vulnerable.

Exercise

How can you actively seek feedback in your job or livelihood?

Do your employer and colleagues have effective ways of giving and receiving feedback? If you are a manager, do you have effective processes in place?

Or:

Seek a different person each day to offer appreciation and praise to.

Share the abundance

"Happiness held is the seed; Happiness shared is the flower."

John Harrigan

There is a kapok tree in Costa Rica that shares its branches with over 4000 different species. Every night it offers up 21 pints (10 litres) of nectar to bats who travel for many miles to come for a drink. In doing so it offers the best bar in town! Of course the kapok gets its flowers pollinated by the bats, but in my view hosting 4000 species does go above and beyond what it needs to survive. The kapok is part of something far bigger than itself and contributes to the great abundance of life.[1]

In our industrial societies things are quite different – success is measured by accumulating wealth and keeping it for ourselves. But in reality, it's exhausting trying to protect what we have, to ensure we have more than we need, and to be on a constant conveyor belt in an attempt to have as much or more than others. Switching your mindset to emulate nature is empowering – you can step off the treadmill that keeps many people heading in a direction they didn't intend.

Step one is to find value in non-monetary and non-material things, and to share them. Compassion, generosity, kindness and empathy all come without financial strings – as do sharing knowledge, experience and skills. If you know how to knit, or grow vegetables, or build a website then find a way to share that. Don't keep it to yourself.

Joanna Macy outlines another way of sharing:

"When you recognize a quality in a person and you name it, you help that person bring it about."[2]

Actively look for the good in others and let them know that you can see value in what they do, and what qualities and talents they have – they will then have the confidence to put into action the great things they have the potential to do.

If you are better off financially than others, recognise that. Share that money around. If you are well-off, it's likely that you have had a leg-up by means of some kind of beneficial factor, like supportive parents, financial stability, a neighbourhood free of violence, or simply food on the table. Whichever way you've come by your money, share it around, for the benefit of the whole, like nature does. Be realistic about what you do have. I know so many well-off people who consider themselves to be financially struggling. We are so used to judging ourselves by what we don't have, we forget the amazing things that we do have. When we only concentrate on the scarcity, we can never be happy or satisfied.

If you have the means, become a pioneer or an early adopter. Many people buy electric cars, not simply because they want to reduce carbon emissions (or for a super quiet ride) – but because they recognise that they are in a privileged position to buy a slightly more expensive car to encourage the technology to move forward, so that others can access it sooner. Early adopters in the tech market pay over the odds and are envied. Fans queue overnight to buy the latest gadget. They take the risk that this might not be the technology that endures. The same should apply to environmental solutions. People who have the time or the money will enjoy them first and these early adopters can also feel good because they are bringing into being new ideas to benefit everyone.

When it comes to sharing, it is ironic that it's those people with lower incomes that donate a higher percentage of their income to charities.[3] If you are more affluent then consider whether you can give more than you do already. Is it possible that you are using unconscious excuses for inaction? Uncomfortable question, I know.

Conversely, if you feel you are not in a position right now to share (perhaps you have health problems or are struggling to afford the basics), then don't feel guilty about it. As Theodore Roosevelt said:

"Do what you can, with what you have, where you are".

Wouldn't it be great if our economic systems could be like a giant network of mycorrhiza acting as a leveller, redistributing wealth? In nature all of this adds up to more abundance, unlike the effects of an extreme capitalist system which creates unequal societies and believes that entrepreneurs and people running companies will work harder only if there are vast differences in wealth. Are the CEOs of the top 100 FTSE British companies really so out of touch with reality that they won't work for less than 400 times the earnings of someone working hard on minimum wage?[4] In a forest, if one tree took many times more than it needed, and left its surrounding trees lacking, then the health of the whole would suffer. Many companies avoid such extremes of inequality by being not-for-profit or by sharing their profits with workers rather than purely shareholders. The pay of the highest earners can be pegged to that of the lowest. We could see mycorrhiza as a sort of redistributing taxation – for a healthier system, companies should carry out their civic duty not to avoid tax, as many of the large multinationals do.

Equal societies are happier ones too.[5] Trust, cohesion, altruism, civic participation, better health, and lower homicide rates are among the results. If you want a demonstration of the divisive power of inequality, try giving one child 400 toys for her birthday and her sister just one. Stand back and watch the fireworks!

Finally, it's important to remember that if we are going to regenerate our wonderful planet and tackle the biggest issues of our time – climate change and ecocide – we will have to share more equitably with other living beings too. Albert Einstein wisely stated that our task must be to:

"widen our circle of compassion to embrace all living creatures and the whole of nature".

The solutions are out there and we have the capacity as humans to pursue them – and I am certainly not going to complain when the side-effect is that we are happier as a result.

Exercise

How can you turn your mindset of not having enough into a mindset of abundance? How much have you got to share? Are you better off financially than others? List your skills, experience and knowledge. How can you share what you have?

Group 5 Principles

Resilience

Develop resilience

"Good timber does not grow with ease; the stronger the wind,
the stronger the trees."

J. Willard Marriott

When it comes to resilience, our tree cousins are masters. They are undoubtedly our best teachers, having developed numerous tactics over hundreds of millions of years. Fortunately, we can speed up our own journey towards resilience by employing many of their methods.

The definition of resilience is to be able to bounce back after difficult experiences, such as trauma, or significant stress. All trees demonstrate resilience – they all cope with wind, changes in temperature, varying levels of rain, and invasions by pests and diseases. Depending on their habitat, trees of different species can survive being scorched, parched, frozen, poisoned by toxins or salt, struck by lightning, eaten, irradiated, maimed, damaged, or cut to the ground. When I think about those traumas I feel inspired to develop strategies to overcome my own troubles, feeling that they are minor in comparison!

Being resilient is not about being tough enough not to feel distress or emotions. A tree may not have nerves, but it 'feels' a limb being struck by lightning nonetheless (or else it wouldn't make the effort to heal over the wound). One of the most resilient trees on the planet was a ginkgo that survived just one mile from the Hiroshima nuclear blast in 1945. I'm sure it didn't do so without experiencing significant internal trauma.

For ourselves, we must acknowledge the pain and sadness that trauma brings and recognise that it is part of the process of recovery. Hurt will be with us along the journey after trauma, rather than being a single hurdle at the start to jump over before we can move on. If this applies to you, examine each emotion so that it doesn't transform into anger, denial, rage or frustration. Remember that a tree strives to be productive rather than paralysed. In the same way, we should use our emotions as a spur to action rather than letting ourselves become frozen.

Everyone has the capacity for resilience inside of them – it's not something you either have or don't have. And often the most resilient people are not those you might expect. Strong athletes with gold medals often face major struggles when their career ends. Conversely, I have worked with victims of sexual exploitation, young girls, who astounded me with their courage and ability to rebuild their lives once they escaped from their traffickers and were given appropriate support.

Becoming more resilient involves effort (like everything in this book!). Setting yourself up with firm roots and investing in your wellbeing is important, as we've discussed. Create 'buffer zones' and 'windbreaks' by building an environment around you that is protective and nurturing. And, when things have gone well, store the results of the 'harvest' for next time, keeping your 'energy bank account' in the black, with deposits of time, friendships, happiness and knowledge. Developing self-belief and courage will give you the confidence that you will succeed when you are knocked back. Over time you can build a network of skills that build across a range of areas, so that, just as for a tree, if one branch gets damaged you have others to nourish you, and the knowledge that you can grow more when you need them.

However well prepared you are, problems will strike out of the blue, like a freak storm, so there's no point in blaming yourself for being unprepared when they do. Having an optimistic outlook is shown to aid 'boucebackability'. My role models for this are eucalyptus trees, which may be ravaged by fire but use that as an opportunity for re-growth of themselves, and germination of their offspring. Those seedlings seize the new opportunities that change brings.

Remember that true resilience involves facing the challenges of the world (and your world) head-on rather than trying to ignore them, or engaging in denial, which is a natural response when things get tough. We are living in challenging times and we all need to build our resilience in order to weather the problems that we're facing, and those to come. We must develop the strength not only to bounce back, but in the process create a better place to bounce back to. Think of the forests of giant redwoods that stood before the Alps or the Rocky Mountains existed. They didn't survive without standing tall and carrying on, adapting and thriving, and making the most of new opportunities.

Case study

Eleanor shared with me her story of resilience.

"I recently got divorced following my husband's betrayal. It was something I never expected to happen. This was a life-changing experience, I was destroyed emotionally and suffered from mental health issues as a consequence. At the time I could not comprehend that my life would ever be better than the happy condition that was my marriage and family.

I'd exhausted many resources in my desperate position – professional, family and friends. The real turning point for me came when I realised I needed to stop looking for other people to be my crutch.

I turned to nature for some lessons on how I could grow as a person to be strong on the inside again, to be more resilient, and for developing the strength I needed in facing an uncertain future. Looking at the principles of nature and what it teaches us, nature's resilience simply told me that nature will always find a way.

I felt that developing resilience was crucial to getting me up and running again and to guarantee my success for thriving. I did a lot of self-help work like cognitive behavioural therapy, meditation, self-reflection etc, to realise that like nature, adaptation is key.

What skills had I had previously for coping? I had been a strong woman. Yes, I had been destroyed, but I could be a strong woman again, but this time better, wiser, and more "bendy with the wind" to meet the new challenges I faced. I saw my new situation as a life just beginning, and like nature, who knows where it may take me. I felt that reflecting on how nature always finds a way – meant that I could too."

Exercise

Take a walk outside and discover the various ways that nature demonstrates resilience.

List the ways that you can learn from them.

What buffers have you created to help you weather storms? How can you develop a positive outlook? Are you prepared to face your emotions head-on?

Know that life is a struggle

"Security is mostly a superstition, it doesn't exist in nature."

Helen Keller

You are sitting reading this amidst a 3.8 billion-year struggle for life. 99% of all species that have ever existed have become extinct, and yet life has continued to grow. Your genes have survived by being passed on by billions of ancestors, but even once the two halves of your DNA were living inside your parents you faced odds of 1 in 10 to the power of 2.5 million. That's 10 followed by over 2.5 million zeros! You have already overcome monumental odds to exist, so why would you even consider not giving life your best shot? We have all despaired at one time or another, and asked *"why can't life be easy?"* – and that's totally understandable, but the fact that life isn't easy can't be a reason for giving up, or worse, feeling that life lacks meaning.

Plants already know that life will be a struggle and are hard-wired for that fact. They don't know which years will be good and which bad, but they go to extraordinary lengths to survive and reproduce. The Saguaro cactus that lives in the Sonoran desert in the southern USA produces 14 million seeds in its lifetime, of which only one will grow into a full sized plant.[1] That's the same odds as winning the UK lottery – a real leap of faith.

For us, knowing that life is meant to be a struggle is empowering. We can transform the belief that *'everything always goes wrong'* into an acceptance that *'shit happens'* and, when we acknowledge that fact, we can move on with the job in hand – sowing the remaining 13,999,999 seeds.

Trees remind us that our struggles often make us stronger. Pot-grown trees fed with lots of liquid fertiliser risk growing without the necessary strength in their trunk and roots, making them more vulnerable to storms. Instead, trees in the wild create strong dense wood by growing slowly and steadily. We might compare this to children who are over-indulged by their parents stepping in to solve their every problem, who later find they lack coping skills when they encounter troubles. I had a very good friend who frequently marched round to the parents of her daughter's school-friends to sort out her squabbles. Of course there are times when we should intervene, but mostly we do our children a disservice if we fight their battles for them. Much better to equip them with strong roots, such as self-confidence; and with strategies, such as empathy and communication skills, to overcome their own childhood fallings-out.

Deciduous trees that are brought inside into the warm over winter don't survive, which reminds us that there will be times of the year, or times in our lives, that are supposed to be more challenging than others. Many people find a cold and wet winter difficult, but you will be more resilient to colds and flu if you spend time outdoors rather than simply travelling from a warm home to a heated office via a warm car. Similarly, healthy immune systems need real invaders to fight – our overly sterile home-cleaning methods can encourage our immune systems to find alternative targets in normally benign substances, or inside our own bodies, leading to allergies and auto-immune diseases.

We are so used to the belief in our modern lives that pain is bad that we forget that it has a purpose. Pain is designed to provoke a response – either to prompt you to move away from a harmful stimulus, to encourage you to take action conducive to healing, or to enable you to learn and grow into a more complex being. The story of the hero's journey – of a person overcoming significant struggles to become a better and stronger person, has been told for millennia, and plays out regularly in movies, such as my favourites, *Star Wars* and *The Hunger Games*.

Pain can also be associated with joy, such as in childbirth. I look back on the pain I felt in bringing my children into the world with pride (although with the normal rose-tinted spectacles that our hormones provide). No doubt my husband does too, given that I was leaning against him for hours on end! If we never lean into pain, vulnerability and discomfort how are we going to experience life to the full? Not to mention that it's hard work spending your life running away from all possible risks. My guess is this accounts for the fact that trees are not totally invulnerable, despite their strength. It's simply not worth putting in a lot of extra effort to resist damage, if that affords only marginal gains – vulnerability is energy-saving, and a certain amount of loss are meant to be endured.

Think back to the principle to **use your energy where it can have the most effect**.

If you are struggling to overcome a challenge, be patient and don't expect overnight results. You are unlikely to have to be as patient as the stones of date trees that can wait for up to 2000 years to germinate once the challenge of reaching a hospitable environment has been overcome!

While you are plugging away, acknowledge that to increase your success rate, your failure rate is likely to increase too. Trees like oaks have years when almost all of their acorns are eaten by a myriad of creatures, but they do it anyway, because they have a long-term strategy. Then every few years they have a 'mast' year, when they produce a bumper crop of acorns that effectively overwhelms the acorn-feeders, which cannot possibly eat them all. This means a decent number of acorns survive to germinate. '*Shit happens*', but it's unlikely to happen every year if you keep going.

So, given that life is a struggle, give yourself permission to make mistakes without beating yourself up. It's good to fail, and it's OK to feel like crap for a while when you do. The saying that "*there is no such thing as failure, only a learning opportunity*" may be true (albeit a cliché these days), but it does tend to ignore the fact that failure hurts. And we know that when stuff hurts, it's important to acknowledge the pain before we move on. I often set myself a time limit for feeling sorry for myself when things haven't gone the way I'd have liked (if it's not too big a thing, I usually give myself the rest of the day to wallow). I liken it to a shortened version of an oak tree's dormant period as it gets ready for its mast year. I find it gets it out of my system, so I can be fresh to start the next day. Winston Churchill said "*success is stumbling from failure to failure with no loss of enthusiasm*". When I retreat to bed with the duvet over my head, I like to look at it as stumbling from failure to failure with only a *temporary* loss of enthusiasm.

Don't forget to balance rewarding failure with celebrating your successes – often things do go right (probably more often than we appreciate), and it's important to throw a 'party' for yourself from time to time (even if it's just a little jig on the spot!). We often recognise and appreciate other people's achievements but forget to celebrate our own hard work. We are conditioned by our culture that acknowledging our own achievements is 'arrogant', but when we do so, we model that

155

behaviour for others, and allow them to appreciate themselves too. No-one likes it when someone implies that they achieved success because they are somehow better than another person, but it is quite different to praise the *effort* that has propelled them there.

Sometimes looking to our accomplishments can help overcome uncomfortable emotions. I was speaking recently to a friend who had been unexpectedly filled with envy because her colleague had achieved something she herself had previously set out to do (but had been prevented from achieving due to ill-health). Someone else then helped her to appreciate the role she had played in her colleague's success. This allowed her to move on from her feeling of jealousy and strengthen their relationship.

Finally, remember that **there are no straight lines** in the living world. Fractal patterns (wobbly lines) are more efficient. They allow living things to move round objects and test new ground. As you walk through life there will be bends in your journey, rocks and bumps in the road, setbacks, horse-shoe bends and enforced pauses, but if you expect them, you can learn to enjoy the view. Keep your purpose in life strong, take decisive actions, and plan for a winding route as you journey through life.

Exercise

List the struggles you are facing at the moment. Do you have an inner voice criticising yourself or blaming other people? Set yourself a time limit for how long you are going to feel sorry for yourself. Then challenge yourself to pick yourself back up.

Bend with the wind

"Notice that the stiffest tree is most easily cracked, while the bamboo or willow survives by bending with the wind."

Bruce Lee

We often learn the hard way that there will be things that we can't control – even mighty oaks experience hurricanes that strike out of the blue and shake their foundations. Feeling out of control is often at the root of many people's frustrations, feelings of failure, anxiety, and relationship problems. Those living with obsessive-compulsive disorder (OCD) or eating disorders often identify this as a cause of their problems. Domestic abuse frequently involves elements of controlling behaviour, which is devastating for the person experiencing it.

There are few shortcuts to overcoming these emotions – they have deep-rooted psychological, emotional and social causes; but perhaps we can learn from trees. For them, wind is a phenomenon that, however hard they might try, they can't totally control. Instead they have developed strategies to cope with gales (or even benefit from them), rather than putting up solid barriers that would pitch them against one of the strongest forces on Earth. For example, leaves and branches leave gaps that allow flows of air to pass through, lessening their impact – quite the opposite of many architect-designed walls that funnel the air up, over and around, creating eddies, frost pockets and wind tunnels. Solid barriers may even cause the wind to push the wall right over.

For us as people that means allowing our stresses and self-defeating thoughts to flow through us. We can acknowledge them so they become less intimidating, and then visualise them passing through our branches and flowing into a river behind us. If you practice meditation or mindfulness you will know that the aim is not to block what's going on in your mind but to encourage thoughts not to linger too long.

Developing a thicker skin may be tempting (and of course necessary in some circumstances), but it can keep good things out, like intimacy and love. Trees have thick bark, but their tough outer skin also contains lenticels – holes that allow them to

157

breathe. They are points of vulnerability but they are the price to pay for life!

Sometimes we are so burdened down with worries that we feel an enormous weight on our shoulders – take inspiration from spruce trees covered in snow that angle their branches purposely downwards in winter to let the snow fall off. Amazingly, they angle their branches to support each other too.

When we do encounter troubles it would be wonderful to be like a young rowan tree that can be bent right to the ground and ping back up – the ultimate in bouncebackability! The lesson from the rowan is when you are lying face down in the mud, turn your head to look back up at the sky!

Sometimes when life gets tough you just have to let go of something important, as if you were dropping a branch. Some trees do this on purpose, like the jack pine. Instead of hanging on to branches that are no longer needed, they actively drop them as an act of self-protection against fire, which could use them to gain a footing upwards. We might learn from this to let go of a relationship that is no longer working or a career move that just hasn't worked out. It's positively beneficial to let go of a relationship that is already causing you harm, like the London plane trees that shed bark to get rid of soot, allowing them to breathe again. Give yourself permission to miss the thing that you have lost (as I'm sure the tree does when it loses a major limb), but not so much that it prevents you from moving on. Use the learning you have gained to fertilise the ground beneath you.

At other times you may simply have to let life take its course and **let it go where it wants to go**. Relinquish control and see where your journey takes you.

Case study

Jo shared his struggles with anxiety.

"I've lived with anxiety at varying levels for a long time and have tried many therapies and techniques, some of which have been really helpful and some not so much. A few months ago I decided to make an effort to switch my focus from expecting someone else to provide the answers and to take control of the situation. The main way I did that was to try to get to know myself better and to spend time looking at how I reacted in different circumstances.

Most of the time I am OK and then something sets me off and I circle into this spiral of self-doubt, and feeling that I'm dying, although the doctors tell me I'm perfectly healthy. In the past I would get angry and frustrated and blame myself for being pathetic, but now I've learned to go with it, to accept that some stress is a natural part of life. I use breathing exercises to help with the immediate physical effects, and then remind myself that if I wait a while it will pass."

Exercise

Take up meditation or mindfulness. Learn how to let thoughts flow through you while you are meditating. See if you can bring this practice into your daily life.

Creatively respond to change

"When the winds of change blow, some people build walls, other people build windmills."

Unknown

The Siberian larch must take the prize for the most adaptable tree. It survives in locations that have temperature differences of up to 100°C (185°F). These deciduous conifers have anti-freeze mechanisms in their trunk and leaves, and they grow 30 m tall in southern Siberia but only 5 m tall around the Arctic Circle. In northern latitudes, where sunlight comes from the side rather than above, the narrow conical shape of conifers maximises the amount of light falling on the leaves. All trees must adapt to their surroundings, either to changing conditions within their lifetimes, or over generations (via natural selection) – diverse species survive in the Arctic, deserts, salt water, high altitudes, full sunlight and dense shade.

One certainty is that **life moves**, and that makes it exciting but somewhat scary for us. When my illness reared its head, it became clear that I would no longer be able to do the physical outdoor work that I had previously loved. It was like a grieving process to let go of aspects of my old life. When my health started to improve, I realised that I had to look for different ways to spend my time. Here I am enjoying writing a book, and sharing my experience with others – neither of which were previously on my (somewhat lengthy!) to-do list. I'm happier than I've ever been – adaptability has been tough mentally but rewarding.

Charles Darwin remarked of nature:

"It is not the strongest of the species that survive, nor the most intelligent, but the one most responsive to change."

I now know that I don't have to be in perfect health, but simply well adapted to the life that I have and that I can create.

Resilience isn't always about bouncing back to your former state. Many people say that a life-changing trauma or illness gave them the opportunity to reflect on what is truly important in life and to change direction as a result. Psychologist

Professor Fausto Massimini's studies on people with paraplegia found that they had clearer goals, a clarity of purpose, and that their disability reduced the contradictory and inessential choices they had previously faced.[1] If you've ever hit rock bottom and fought your way back up it becomes a source of confidence and strength.

As creative, adaptable, human beings we have an evolutionary advantage. We can create a better life for ourselves, and for others, more rapidly that other species, who can often only adapt through generational evolutionary processes. Humans are the most adaptable species on Earth, thanks to the ways our brains and our hands have developed in tandem. We can take on information and learn new skills within minutes rather than generations. We can set goals and work towards them to improve our lot. We have adapted to all regions of the planet – even more so than trees, who can't survive on the highest mountain-tops or in the Arctic Circle. All of these adaptations occur at a vastly more accelerated rate than evolution by means of DNA would allow on its own.

But our adaptability brings threats as well as opportunities. In the same way as our good choices can lead to great things, like curing disease or creating musical masterpieces, our bad decisions have consequences too, such as making nuclear bombs and burning fossil fuels.

Our personal choices can have almost instant consequences – donate to charity and your money will be used to buy water purification in a disaster zone within days or hours. Invest in a pension that funds arms deals or tobacco (most do, read the small print) and your money will be sent off in an entirely different direction.[2]

Our challenge is to not ignore the harsh realities of life that we would naturally rather not think about, such as how our decisions impact on other people's way of living, cause pollution and harm the rest of the living world. Instead we can adapt in a positive way, making the right choices after gathering as much information as we can.

Many aspects of our societies are created from myths that were devised by humans. These include nation states, business models, financial and economic systems, philosophies and belief systems. Money, for example, is simply the trust that when you

161

give me a piece of paper I will provide a physical item or a service to you in return (or alternatively give you more money in the form of interest). When that trust breaks down, the paper becomes worthless as we see in countries experiencing hyper-inflation. Similarly, nation states are not separated by concrete boundaries but by lines drawn on maps with the shared belief that those lines represent differences – and humans have then created consequent physical manifestations (such as laws, governments and border controls) for these beliefs. The excellent book *Sapiens: A Brief History of Humankind* by historian Yuval Noah Harari explains this concept in detail, and sets out its origins in the human 'cognitive revolution' that happened around 70,000 years ago.[3] The point of including this in a book about learning from trees is to remind ourselves that these are not immutable laws of the universe (such as gravity and electromagnetic radiation are) and therefore if these social constructs have been made, they can be un-made, or adapted to our current needs. We have the potential (if we have the collective will) to transform ourselves and our societies via relatively rapid revolutionary rather than purely evolutionary means. This is done by encouraging new ways of thinking, and by looking for solutions by different means from those that created the problems in the first place. I'm not shying away from the enormity of the task, but a critical mass of people could lead a culture change – and would do so much more rapidly than the 500-year generational cycles that evolutionary DNA offers a forest.

Sometimes it's best not merely to adapt but to hasten a 'positive disintegration'[4] so that we can re-make our systems better adapted next time – annual flowers do this when they return to a seed every year and re-grow with (sometimes substantial) modifications. In our societies this gives opportunities for healthier systems but also helps to create more cultural and psychological diversity, and the hybrid vigour that comes with it. The creation of the modern welfare state in the UK between 1945 and 1951 is one example – its architects looked at existing healthcare, but instead of modifying it slightly, decided to create an entirely new system.

We can learn from nature that **a bare space will always be filled**. When wild boars root up the ground-cover layer of a forest floor looking for food, patches of ground open up. But these don't stay bare for long – nature will rapidly move in. These spaces are great opportunities for new life. For us, it might be a redundancy that creates new openings, or a house move into an unfamiliar neighbourhood. However, we have to make sure we are filling that space with good things before the pernicious weeds move in. On a day-to-day level, filling a bare space means using your time productively, whether it be in work, creativity or leisure, rather than letting the couch-potato weeds move in.

In trees, genetic mixing can result in beneficial, deleterious or neutral effects in the offspring – and our choices each have the same potential outcomes. The problem for us is that the effects of our bad choices don't necessarily have a chance to become extinct before the next terrible decision comes along. The overall effect is that we have the potential to create lives that are compounding bad decision on top of bad decision – unless we make a conscious effort to make the next decision a good one after all. Because many bad decisions add up to catastrophic ones on a global scale, we have a duty to ensure that our day-to-day evolutions (choices) result in beneficial outcomes for us and our world.

One way to be better adapted in your personal life is to **remain flexible** in your thinking. Design your life so that you can respond to change when it happens. Most people nowadays will have 'portfolio careers' – many jobs in their lifetime – unlike their grandparents, so it's important to develop transferable skills. Value and learn from all of your experiences, however much you might have disliked them at the time. I'm sure my son is learning about empathy, patience and dignity, while wiping bottoms and talking to people with dementia in a care home. These will be valuable life lessons whatever career he chooses. Whether we like it or not, many jobs are gradually being given to robots and AI, so we should encourage our children to develop the skills that require human talents. These include critical thinking, problem-solving, written and verbal communication, and creativity. Sadly, instead, many schools seem stuck in Victorian times, asking pupils to learn facts that can be found at the touch of a screen, or which may soon become out of date.

One way to overcome challenges is with **solutions thinking** – focusing on the solution rather than the problem.[5] It is empowering to believe that each problem does have a solution. However, to start with you will probably need to spend a bit of time working out what the problem actually is. This is usually the most challenging part of the process, and you may find it's not what you think. For example, it's possible that someone finding it difficult adapting to life as a new mum may actually be experiencing a delayed bereavement over the loss of their own parent. Or someone nervous of a promotion may actually be worrying about the commitment they have to their aged father.

When you are looking for solutions it can be of benefit to look for the most logical one. Occam's razor is a problem-solving principle theorising that simpler solutions are more likely to be correct than complex ones. I adopted this principle when trying to persuade doctors (in many different disciplines) that I didn't have 15 different problems (which was approximately the number of diagnoses I had), but just one or two that accounted for all of my symptoms. It seemed logical to me, but unfortunately no doctor in 30 years was able to think beyond the list of illnesses that they had learned in medical school. One wonderful General Practitioner eventually had the courage to say *"you have one illness but I don't know what it is "*, which paved the way to obtaining the diagnosis of a rare disease. And once I knew what the problem was (via the diagnosis) I got to work on the solution.

While you are finding the problem, don't mull over it for too long, as it's all too easy to be dragged into melancholy and pessimism. If you have a big problem to solve, intersperse it with more pleasurable activities that keep you going. Remember the aim is **action, not inaction**.

Once you've worked out what the problem actually is, you can look for solutions in different ways. First of all, don't hang around people who, as Einstein put it, *"have a problem for every solution "*. They can definitely sap your energy. I see this on environmental forums all the time when someone comes up with a great idea and others (who presumably also want positive change for the world) come up with 100 oppositional *"but what abouts..."*. They probably don't think they are doing anything wrong but it undermines progress rather than encourages it. A recent example was criticism of the marches drawing attention to climate change, on the grounds that many disabled people found it difficult to join in. The critics were supportive of the aims of the march, but the overall effect was that heart-sink moment when you can see the potential for a movement to splinter because of the very people who could be supporting it. They can't see the demoralising effect on everyone, not just the organisers, who are doing their best. When we looked at the principles in Group 1, we talked about the benefits of seeing the big picture, and here is a prime example. It would be much more helpful to acknowledge the aims of the climate march and add a solution on top of their solution, that addresses the issue raised. That's the way that nature would approach it, creating more upon more.

There are many creative ways of finding solutions. Lateral thinking, coined by Edward de Bono, looks for creative and indirect approaches rather than step-by-step logic.[6] Elephant remains dating back 120,000 years have been found very near my home, on the banks of the river Trent.[7] When faced with these elephants, the logical approach of the native trees back then might have been to put a lot of energy into strengthening their roots and trunk, but the creative approach (adopted by many trees) was to develop mechanisms that allow themselves to be browsed and even cut right down, but to re-grow stronger once the herd had moved on. These include oak, ash, beech, hornbeam, hazel and willow. When my family and I coppice trees in our own woodland, which involves cutting them close to the ground, I like to think of elephants hundreds of thousands of years ago leading the way. Woodworkers have, for thousands of years, benefitted from the trees' creative ability to re-grow stronger and healthier. Communities harvest craft materials on regular cycles from coppiced woodlands that, when well maintained, last much longer than their non-coppiced counterparts.

Solutions thinking is empowering and exciting. I enjoy the challenge of looking at the world from different perspectives, with the knowledge that there is always some kind of solution. Many people (including me) have agonised for decades about the problems of environmental crises and why things are getting worse rather than better. It's easy to become frustrated and demoralised, or to blame others for greed or laziness. By turning the problem on its head, you realise that one of the primary problems is that we are divorced from the natural world. We are being harmed by that disconnection, so we are harming the living things around us. Armed with that knowledge, the solution then becomes more obvious – reconnect with nature, heal ourselves, and then we will protect the living world as something we love.

Exercise

List the problems you are facing right now. Try to develop a solution-orientated mentality. Write three potential solutions for each problem. Make one of the solutions a 'wild' one.

Seek and offer support

*"Trees are much like human beings and enjoy each other's company.
Only a few love to be alone."*

Jens Jensen

When trauma strikes, having a network of family and friends to draw on has been shown to make a tremendous difference to resilience.[1] Forests teach us that having a variety of supportive relationships, where each individual can communicate their needs, is a long-term predictor of health and recovery.

Don't be afraid to ask for help. Being too strong doesn't help you or the other people around you. Even the strongest pine tree will enlist the help of thousands of ladybirds when it is attacked by aphids. It does this by sending out a request for help in the form of a perfume.

Be specific – most friends and family members want to help but often don't know what to do. It may be that coming to do some cleaning or picking up the shopping is more useful than sitting with you and talking. Other days you may just need a shoulder to cry on. If you are the one offering support think about what the person actually needs, or whether you are adding more strain into an already difficult situation. It sounds terribly ungrateful, but when I was at my worst my heart sank when someone turned up with flowers that I had to arrange. It felt like climbing Everest just to find a vase.

A long-lasting 'perennial' system of friends (to use a horticultural term) will be more able to support you than here-today-gone-tomorrow 'annual' friends. Having said that, you might be surprised at who steps up. Some people are more willing or able than others to help those in need, and those who show the most empathy will often be people who themselves have experienced hard times.

Friends who can listen are more helpful than those who simply tell you what you *should* do, or what worked for them. Be open to the wisdom that they bring, but remember that you must find your own path and your own tools for recovery.

Difficult emotions – like guilt, shame or the desire not to burden others – may lead someone who you would like to help to withdraw. Depression can certainly cause this response, I know. At its extreme the feeling of being a burden to others can lead to the belief that everyone is better off without you. That feeling has no basis in fact, but the person feeling it believes it completely.

In the past I have tried to overcome the feeling of guilt for burdening others by knowing that, once I am well, I can 'pass it on' by helping someone else when they are most in need; and indeed that opportunity arose when an acquaintance had a breakdown. I didn't know her well and didn't expect anything in return for my help, but I hope that now she is well, she will continue the positive spiral by helping a friend or stranger when they need it.

Something nature teaches us is to **work from yourself outwards**. A tree will ensure that it has a strong taproot and a strong trunk, then strong branches, then strong leaves, next strong friends (trees and other species), and finally strong surroundings. All are important, but the firm foundations must come first. Feed your roots to ensure you are strong enough to support others.

Psychologist and author Dr Martin Seligman offers a recipe for happiness.[2] Here is a brief summary. We can learn to appreciate and enjoy the basic pleasures of life – those that meet our basic needs, and those that connect us with other people and with the rest of the living world. Next we can examine our unique strengths, use them for a purpose, and develop self-esteem. As part of this process we must learn to value ourselves. Our service to others plays an important part in developing self-esteem and happiness. Third, we must find meaning in something bigger than ourselves, and use our unique strengths to pursue something greater.

You will notice that this recipe for happiness aligns with the tree principles for good living as set out in this book, especially the principles in Group 2 (purpose), Group 4 (connection) and Group 6 (future).

Get to know yourself, build the firm foundations of self-acceptance and self-confidence, and you will be in a much better position to then work outwards to engage with the world – to be an active participant and to support others. There is, of course, a balance to be struck (did I mention that nature likes balance?) – work out the optimal amount of time to spend on you, so you don't get stuck in a self-absorbed spiral of over-thinking at the expense of doing. Conversely, avoid jumping straight into helping others if you have health or emotional needs that might lead to burn-out.

To make a decision about where to put your precious energy, identify what your spheres of influence are. With regard to your own self and your own life, you have a great deal that you can control, but as you move outwards, your ability to affect other people, your environment and beyond reduces considerably. You may be the most significant person in your partner's life but you still can't control their decisions and their reactions. Spend your energy within areas that you can influence – for example, it is wasting your precious energy and creating stress to try to force someone to give up smoking or taking drugs, although you can provide the conditions to support them when they make that decision for themselves. You can't force an acorn to germinate – but you can provide fertile ground for it to do so itself.

It might help to imagine that you have a set of rings or zones around you. Invest in three to five close friends and family members, then work outwards. Then think about your wider networks. Research by anthropologist Robin Dunbar has shown that social cohesion occurs at the level of 150 people maximum.[3] That's the maximum number of people with whom we can maintain individual relationships. That's not to say that we shouldn't try and have influence more widely (we are part of a global economic and social system), but imagine if everyone was in one or more communities of 50–150 around the world, which overlapped and formed giant interconnected ecosystems. Your communities might be the people in the geographical area where you live, and your workplace, organisation, leisure activity group; or a group with a mutual interest online. Think how much more empowered each of us would feel if we were supported and could support others in small communities, actively participating in decision-making. The 150 would then influence 1000, then 1 million, then perhaps 7 billion! And when you look for them, there are already millions of communities around the world doing just that.

While this might be an ideal situation, and I may be labelled as utopian to even suggest it, you can make a start, yourself as an individual. Strengthen your connections with your friends, and then turn to your local community. You can actively participate in your local organisations – anything from joining the local walking club or children's outdoor activity group, to representing your neighbours on the local council. You might want to become an activist and join with others who want to create change, whether it be in the social or ecological sphere – the world certainly needs many more people to take action right now. A critical mass (including young people) is now emerging on climate action, for example.

The most important thing to remember as you work to the edge of your sphere of influence is not to waste energy on worry, frustration or resentment. As Nelson Mandela said, *"resentment is like drinking poison and hoping it will kill your enemies"*. Equally futile is spending any time whatsoever on things that you have no control over – things that happened in the past, the number of hours in the day, things you can't predict, and whether someone you are trying to help will accept your help and advice. Remember the principle **use your energy where it can have most effect** that we talked about in the Group 2 principles.

Make an active decision where you choose to spend your energy. Although your influence declines as you work outwards, you can still make a difference.

Case study

Will told me that a few years ago he was in a really bad place.

"Don't get me wrong, I am very lucky, I know that. I have food to eat, a roof over my head and sufficient income to secure my future. But with things falling apart around me, losing my dad and the love of my now ex, I was falling apart. The roots of my life needed to be healed, nurtured, with sufficient nutrients (love and purpose) to support the tree above, and the branches it extends to support others. I now have a new partner, an established gardening business and am able to have plenty of energy left over to share my time and knowledge with others."

Learn to heal yourself

*"The art of medicine consists of amusing the patient
while nature cures the disease."*

Voltaire

When we explored the principles in Group 3 we talked about the need to invest in your wellbeing. But what do you do when things have gone wrong – when you've had a trauma, setback, illness or injury? How can you help yourself to recover?

Seek out your favourite tree and you'll see it is covered in wounds. From fungi, woodpeckers, rodents, squirrels, wind, rain and from broken branches. Each wound has been carefully healed by instinctive mechanisms. Trees can even heal people (and animals) – for example, salicylic acid is found in willow, but you'll know it as aspirin. Hypericum (St John's wort) is used to treat mild and moderate depression.

Every illness is unique to you – the same illness won't have exactly the same symptoms in one person as another. Because you are an ecosystem, you have a wide variety of organs, systems, genes and processes that will manifest illness in different ways. And for this reason you are the best person to draw all the elements of healing together. You can enlist the help of doctors, complementary therapists, counsellors, friends, family and the internet to support you. A friendly doctor who can help you navigate your way through illness is invaluable – I was lucky enough to find one, after many years of misdiagnosis.

Our bodies have a remarkable process for healing – the immune system. Without it we wouldn't survive in the outside world. Some ways of supporting our immune system include: a diet rich in plant-based foods, seeds, nuts and pulses; ensuring you have adequate vitamins, especially A, C and D; avoiding stress, and getting adequate rest. Studies show that healthy gut bacteria also play a key role in immune system health. Laughing and singing help too. (You could join a choir to do both at the same time!) In case you are wondering, trees do have a rudimentary immune system that protects from invaders, although it is not nearly as complicated as ours.[1]

Healing is a holistic process – whatever your illness or injury, aim to nourish your body and your mind. Our brains are evolved to spend one-third of our time asleep, so it pays to make sleep a priority. Having a healthy sleep routine might involve turning off your screens two hours before bedtime; and a warm bath with calming essential oils can help too. Getting outside early in the morning stimulates the pineal gland, which has a regulating effect on both circadian (daily) and seasonal sleep patterns – yet more proof that being in nature is good for you. A 2016 study conducted in Finland and Austria demonstrated that birch trees have a circadian rhythm and 'sleep' at night – they relax their branches (and thereby conserve energy) – so you'll be in good company.[2]

A close second priority on the recovery front is diet – you are unique, so find the right diet for you. It is likely that will be a balanced, primarily plant-based diet, but many people with specific illnesses find that specialist diets can help.

Exercise is important too. The last thing you'll fancy doing when you're unwell is getting outside and doing exercise (exercise is better done outside if at all possible), but often you'll feel better for even a short trip out. And you may also obtain your fix of vitamin D in the process. Employ the trees to help nurse you back to health – one study has even demonstrated that simply seeing nature through a hospital window could speed up recovery times.[3]

In psychological terms, expect healing to be a messy process. Television programmes often portray courageous people 'battling' against illness and disability. We often only see a sanitised version of recovery that has edited out all the times that the person would cheerfully thump their carer for bringing the wrong strength of tea – as well as all the times the heroic carer has cried uncontrollably at the unrelenting nature of their tasks. In my experience, recovery can be full of frustration and resentment. To get through it you have to meet those emotions head-on and be tough, dogged and determined to persevere to make things better tomorrow than they are today. And you'll have to balance that with the days when you just want to pull the covers over your head and wish the world would go away. Life is a struggle but 'grit' has been shown to be a key factor in resilience.[4] Take it day by day, listen to your body, and let nature play its part in supporting you to heal.

Exercise

Design a plan to get well or to live more healthily.

- Start with the observations you discovered when we explored the Group 1 principles. Look at every aspect of your life.
- List your symptoms. Look at all parts of your body and your mind. Don't ignore symptoms you think are unrelated to your main issue. Remember that all your body systems are connected.
- Then work out all the resources you have to help you (medicine, complementary therapies, friends, family, food, exercise, green spaces etc).
- Next list the things that might limit your recovery (finances, work, time constraints, family commitments etc).
- Do your research, gather information.
- Change only one thing at a time. Keep a diary to track any changes.
- Listen to any feedback that your body is giving you.
- Make the next changes one at a time.

Tune in to natural cycles

"Let us learn to appreciate that there will be times when the trees will be bare, and look forward to the time when we may pick the fruit."

Anton Chekhov

Sadly, many people now live divorced from the natural world, and move through a year barely knowing the cycles of the seasons. I am sometimes surprised to find, if I comment about a lack of rain to someone I bump into, that they have no idea it hasn't rained for days. Each year a handful of people ring up the Forestry Commission in distress to report that the leaves on the trees in their local areas have shrivelled up and gone brown. They are then politely told that it's a concept called 'autumn' which has been happening for quite a long time and is nothing to worry about!

We evolved, for the most part, while we lived outdoors, and our bodily systems still operate according to the revolving timescales of our planet. Sunlight regulates our body clock and this has implications not only for sleep but for the regulation of hormones, and therefore for all the body's functions. Similarly, menstrual cycles follow a regular, monthly pattern – and listening to the changes in body and emotions during the cycle can lead to improved body-awareness and thus wellbeing.

When we try to override the seasons and adopt the same lifestyles all year round, our bodies and our minds can suffer. We did not evolve to be office workers, going to work in the dark and coming home after sunset.

Nature illustrates that it's healthy to **take time to pause**. The biggest mass pause on the planet occurs in the temperate zones encircling the globe, when autumn colours give way to winter dormancy. In my own life, I now love and appreciate autumn and winter as a time for rest and rejuvenation, whereas when I was younger I experienced them only as dullness – a time that I spent mourning the loss of summer and waiting impatiently for the start of spring. Remember that taking a rest when you need it isn't laziness or wasted time – so it's not worth feeling guilty or frustrated. Once we can see dormancy as a regenerative process, and know that after winter comes spring, we can relax while looking forward to making the most of the rising sap and the energy that new growth brings. I know that I feel exhilarated in spring and feel that I 'wake up' in sync with my garden.

Other types of breaks might include a gap year after the stress of exams, taking a sabbatical from work, having an extended holiday, or plucking up the courage to tell your boss that you've worked so many days overtime that you're going to take those days off in lieu (I know many people who don't even take their allocated days holiday from work, such are the pressures of modern life). Of course if you are able to get off the treadmill altogether then there will be more time to take life at the pace it was designed for – slow rhythmic work interspersed with periods of intense activity, just like our hunter–gatherer ancestors and our forest cousins.

Plan to pause each day – with relaxation, mindfulness, outdoor activity, or whatever you find works for you. When you get to know your body it will tell you when you need to give yourself a break. We all know that feeling of going through the motions at work because our heart's not in it, or we're exhausted. Flexible employment practices help if they allow you to work when your energy and creativity are at their highest.

When pause is seen as a valuable and temporary process (one that will naturally come to an end) there is less desire to 'drop out'. Pausing is to be embraced, something to gravitate towards, not something you come to only when you burn out or can no longer face the world. If we all learned to pause before the point of no return, without feelings of guilt, then we could live more happily and more productively. Inspired by the cycles of breathing, remember that you must make time for breathing in and for breathing out – you can't breathe out all of the time.

Remember that pause can be a time to harness the power of cycles to create momentum. When a seed is dormant it has all the potential to become a mighty tree, but it waits patiently for the right conditions. It must make sure its timing is right, balanced between waiting long enough for the warmth but not hesitating too long, so it can ride the surge of ideal conditions for maximum benefit. Ride the wave of energy after a pause and you'll find that a job that you had been putting off for months gets done in an afternoon.

Pauses in nature can lead to wondrous transformations. One of the most beautiful sites in a British woodland – a blanket of bluebells that have laid dormant in their bulbs all winter – is particularly magnificent because the burst of colour as the flowers open en masse is synchronised to happen before the leaf canopy closes above. The metamorphosis of a butterfly pupa is another example of a pause leading to a transformation. I love the saying *"There is nothing in a caterpillar that tells you it is going to be a butterfly"* – without the dull cocoon phase, the vivid colours fluttering in the breeze would not come into existence. We don't call the bluebell bulbs or the pupating butterfly lazy, so we shouldn't put that label on ourselves or others when we pause to rejuvenate, as long as we commit to engaging with the subsequent burst of activity.

Another way that we can learn from nature's cycles is to know that any bad phase in our life **will not last** – the cycle will come around eventually, just like spring coming after winter. Just holding on to that idea can help in gaining the courage to carry on.

However, while difficult phases won't last, good phases sadly often don't endure either. In the highs, we can enjoy the good times but can try to even out the bumps so we don't come crashing down. Save for a rainy day by putting money aside. Invest in transferable skills so that you have a fall-back (or fall-forwards!) option. Better still, create a lifestyle that requires little income when times change – being off-grid or living in a house with almost no heating or electricity bills is achievable and has benefits for your own resilience and for the rest of the living world.

In modern life we are being sold the 'dream' that we should always be striving for more and more growth – whereas in fact 'enough' would make us all happier. By examining the predator and prey cycles (like the ebb and flow of wolf, elk and trees) we can see that healthy systems don't enjoy unsustainable growth. Elk browse on trees and if unrestrained will cause lasting damage to the tree populations, but if wolves are present, they not only prey on the deer, but move them on, allowing the trees time to regenerate. If the wolves kill too many elk, wolf numbers will fall due to lack of food, then tree health will flourish. With increased food, deer populations will rise again, then wolves come along and so the cycle continues. A fascinating example of this balancing act can be observed in Yellowstone National Park, where willow and aspen populations have recovered (with a host of knock-on benefits) since wolves were reintroduced in 1995 after an absence of 60 years.[1] A healthy ecosystem will balance itself out, preventing runaway consumption. More doesn't equal better, as we will no doubt find out, either by waiting for the current runaway trajectory of consumption to come to its inevitable end, or by putting in place regenerative alternatives that do work, some of which you will find in the next group of principles.

We see unhealthy cycles in economic systems too – those that lack regulatory mechanisms to bring them back into balance. Successive governments across the globe have failed to implement mechanisms that would avoid each extreme peak and each extreme trough, such as those in housing markets, stock markets and inflation. One former prime minister of the UK famously said *"no more boom and bust"* right up until the economic crash of 2008. Perhaps he should have spent longer looking at the changing seasons and less time looking at spreadsheets.

The optimal way you can learn from nature's cycles is the direct way – to get outside each and every day, and walk in the woods or in your local park. Turn off your phone and tell your mind that you'd like it to go quiet for a while. Observe the changing seasons: see the detail on a leaf as it turns brown and falls; feel the icy cold on your face during a crisp winter day; crouch down and see the green shoots of the bulbs pushing through the brown earth in spring; experience the short-lived colourful display of wildflowers in summer; appreciate the beauty of transient autumn colours and recognise that its beauty comes precisely because it doesn't last. When you allow yourself to experience the cycles of nature, your body will tell you how it wants you to live.

Case study

Sally shared her experience of learning from natural cycles.

"As I get older, I'm learning more and more about the important life lessons we can learn from observing and mimicking nature. I've been experimenting with using cyclical patterns in how I run my business and I am gradually moving away from linear patterns that we are traditionally taught, towards more nature-inspired cyclical patterns.

I had thought that in order to be successful, I had to increase my workload and widen my business reach every year. I thought I had to be consistent and keep on showing up in the world in the same way, day after day, month after month, and year after year. This quickly led me to a crisis point where burn-out was coming ever closer and I was experiencing warning signs of stress, anxiety and exhaustion.

It was time for a change. Nothing in nature stays the same; the moon waxes and wanes, the tree sheds its leaves, the seasons reach an energetic peak with the summer solstice then relax back towards darkness again.

So I decided to apply these cycles to my work life. I looked at my priorities and adapted my workload to accommodate ebbs and flows: time for striving with all my might, balanced with time for rest.

One of the most obvious things I did was follow nature's lead and rest more over the winter months. I chose to not deliver sessions in December, January or February. I work outdoors and these months always felt very hard. Battling the cold, wet and dark was draining my energy and minimising my joy. At this time of year, nature is resting, animals are hibernating and trees are bare of leaves. So by allowing myself these months for rest, I set myself up well for a burst of energy in the spring, when I can re-start my outdoor sessions full of enthusiasm with all the behind-the-scenes work like marketing, planning and paperwork already in place. So I can catch up on lost time and lost income by having vastly renewed my energy over the winter ebb, ready for the spring flow!"

Exercise

What cycles can you observe in your own life? Can you adapt the way you live to become more in tune with nature's rhythms?

Group 6 Principles

Future

Invest in the future

"A society grows great when old men plant trees under whose shade they know they shall never sit."

Unknown

Are you worried about the future? If your answer is yes, then that might be surprisingly good news. Right now we are living in scary times, and those of us who feel anxious about what is to come wield power. We are the ones staring reality in the face and have the motivation and the ability to envisage a better future. BUT there is a big caveat. We have to find ways to transform our fear into action. If we allow it to paralyse us, we are contributing to the problem, not helping to solve it.

As we've seen throughout this book, trees are on a productive and active trajectory, unlike we humans who have the tendency to deny what is going on around us. It takes a mind-shift to think of trees as the proactive ones and we humans as the inactive avoiders.

In our world we need a healthy balance of optimists, pessimists and realists. Each can use our unique way of thinking *to promote change*. We know that pessimists can sometimes be frustrated by optimists because they have a tendency to merrily carry on, blind to the dangers; and optimists can be de-motivated by pessimists whom they see as mood-sapping, preventing them from effecting the necessary changes. Yet if we remain open to the different perspectives the other party brings to a problem, we can work together towards a common goal.

So are trees optimists or pessimists? I would argue that they are both. They are optimistic because they need to continue onwards, whatever life might throw at them, facing unbelievable odds (remember our beech nut with its odds of 1.8 million to one), but they are pessimists because they expect things to go wrong (remember our oak's mast years where it compensates for the years when all its acorns will be eaten). The difference between us and the trees is that trees always use their optimism or pessimism **to spur them into action**.

Another way of looking at trees is as *regeneratists**, and we humans can choose to be regeneratists too – that is, we can be inspired by the ways in which nature can take any manner of past experience and turn it into positive action, regenerating and creating more and more abundance.

*[I've taken the liberty of making this word up to describe an individual with the mentality of regeneration – someone who goes beyond the aims of sustainability (keeping a situation as it is) towards creating more and more from the resources around them, just like nature does. The idea comes from regenerative agriculture, but it has the potential to be used in all spheres of life.]

Evolution has the effect of making all living beings **forward-thinking**. Trees and plants make enormous sacrifices to optimise their reproductive success. Such a sacrifice can be observed in a tree that blossoms and fruits spectacularly in response to life-threatening stress – it puts all its energy into reproducing before the end of its life, and in doing so hastens its demise.

Some trees even nurture their young directly – did you know that mangroves bear live young? Their seeds germinate while still attached to the tree, and only fall once the root and the shoot have grown. But all trees will attempt to provide their offspring with the most ideal conditions that they can in the circumstances – their aim is for their 'children' to survive, regardless of whether they are around to see them grow. As trees reproduce and contribute to the complexity of life, more and more fertile niches are created to support more and more life, and so it goes on. If nature as a whole had consciousness, it would never say *"we're OK, let's leave it at that"*. It keeps on building more and more diversity, creating more and more life, over millions and billions of generations.

In the same way that we can observe these sacrifices in trees, we know that there are millions and millions of incredibly generous people all around the world who spend their time working for future generations, not only for their own children but for other people's children too – including those that they don't know and will never meet. They use their energy and resources, and work hard so their children can have the opportunities they need; they set aside their own desires for those of others, and in extreme circumstances might even risk or sacrifice their life for their children and for other people's children. We witnessed this in World War II, when entire nations made sacrifices for a better future and when many brave people risked themselves (and died) to allow children to escape to freedom. Extreme sacrifices still continue today under oppressive regimes, in war zones, and when refugees struggle to make it across the Mediterranean.

However, when taken as a whole species, we *Homo sapiens* often struggle to think about the effects of our actions on our own generation, let alone any future ones. Our cultural definition of a 'better' life (usually one involving more material wealth and a higher income) is often not better at all, in terms of how that lifestyle affects future generations of people and other living beings. But today there is a rapidly growing percentage of people able to see the wider context of the world our descendants will actually inhabit. We can create a better future by considering the longer term and the bigger picture.

"But", you might say, *"why should I sacrifice myself for future generations of people who I won't know?"* I totally get how scary that sounds. What if I told you that investing in the future isn't a sacrifice? Remember back to the Group 2 principles – where we saw that one of the primary causes of happiness is to **live with purpose**, and, in addition, that purpose will make you happier if you find meaning outside of yourself, and in the service of others. In the principles in Group 5, we talked about people who have bounced back from trauma being happier, because they had a chance to reflect on the important things in life and had thereby found meaning.

I would strongly argue that you can be happier and more fulfilled if you find your purpose in connecting with and dedicating your time to other people and to other living beings. I'm not just making this up – I know it works, because it works for me and for many people I know.

We can extend our purpose to beyond the grave, creating benefits for future generations. And when we do so, it becomes much easier to decouple short-term desires from the real feelings of worth and satisfaction that come from being part of the greatest show on Earth – a global ecosystem that can thrive for millions of years into the future.

As geneticist and environmentalist Wes Jackson said:

"If your life's work can be accomplished in your lifetime you're not thinking big enough".

Our future will not be made better by us all acting as individuals. We are not simply responsible for our own children, but for those of our communities too. And we don't all have to pass on our genes to be deemed a success (just in case you thought that I might be arguing that we all have a duty to procreate; we don't). Consider bees – only one member of a colony (the queen, who mates with several drones from a different colony) will pass on her genes within that hive. That doesn't make the other bees failures. As a 'super-organism' a bee colony ensures the survival of future generations by working together, each with a defined role, and co-operating and communicating on a grand scale. Human societies are 'super-organisms' too – each of us must find our niche to make our communities (small or big) operate successfully. As such, we must put effort into raising other people's children and into creating ideal conditions for future generations.

While it would be great to think that every single member of the human race has the willingness and ability to face the challenge, even in a bee colony there will be a tiny proportion of bees that don't pull their weight – they might seem like shirkers, destructive, or just plain dumb. Our challenge as human populations is to ensure that we have a similarly small proportion of unhelpful or damaging ideas that are taken forward. It is not a contradiction to value the input of each individual while designing out the unproductive or destructive ideas and systems that we have previously relied on.

Furthermore, we must stop thinking of ourselves as the culmination of evolution. There is no straight line with apes at one end and a human at the other end (as might be printed on a T-shirt). We are just a small part of a complex and continuing 3.8 billion-year-old process. We can argue that, being relatively recent in our development, we have not yet demonstrated our resilience long-term. Those bacteria that have survived almost unchanged for hundreds of millions of years surely have one over on us, since they have proved that they are supremely adapted to their environments. Our forward trajectory means that our bodies and our brains will continue to evolve, largely dependent on the choices we now make collectively. These choices might include gene editing, policies on reproduction, business decisions on which products to make, or regulatory decisions on which chemicals or technologies to ban. All of these have the potential to change the future of human beings in the blink of an evolutionary eye. We must establish effective and intelligent processes to decide which are beneficial to take forward.

The interconnectedness of life means that all organisms influence the evolution of those around them, interacting and altering each other by direct contact or by altering the ecosystem in which they live. But we humans are in the unique position of altering the evolution of every single life-form on our planet. Every single one. That has never before happened, either in the history of other creatures or in the history of human beings. It's happening on a global scale with climate change, with ecosystem destruction, and with plastic pollution (which is now even in the deep oceans) and it is one mammoth responsibility. But we know the causes (us), and we know the solutions (including two really obvious ones – stop emitting carbon and sequester it from the air; and stop making, buying and using stuff we don't need). Our challenge is to use our collective capacity for action and innovation to tip the balance back in favour of the creative rather than the destructive, and to allow nature to help us in this endeavour.

Since 2008, Wales has planted one tree for every child born or adopted. If we could plant a tree for every child born throughout the world (around 130 million per year) and then expand that to also plant trees for everyone else (over 7 billion) then we really would be demonstrating that we are investing in the future. Go on, get out there – plant those trees, and make your purpose doing good for your own descendants and those of other species.

Exercise

Are you an optimist, a pessimist or a realist? Is your way of thinking about the future getting in the way of taking action?

Do you consider yourself a regeneratist (someone who plays an active part in creating more and more, like nature does)?

List the ways in which your purpose in life can include creating a better future.

Know that death is part of life

"For life and death are one, even as the river and seas are one."
Khalil Gibran

There are some single-celled organisms that are considered immortal, but all other life-forms on Earth experience death. It is the only certainty of complex life – and it is a price I am certainly willing to pay for the privilege of being a multi-cellular organism.

For me, the knowledge that my body will be recycled into nutrients for other organisms is wonderful. Indeed it's always seemed logical to me that my body contains the stuff of new life. At the age of seven (an age when many children are getting to grips with the ideas surrounding death), I asked my mother if she could bury me on the compost heap when I died (her answer was unsurprisingly, no, in case you were wondering whether I was brought up in some strange cult instead of a conservative middle-class village in England). For me there was nothing more natural than creating fertility with which to feed my beloved plants. Luckily for me, my mother hasn't yet had to confront that reality, but I do still have the desire to have a green burial, surrounded by trees. If all this sounds rather romantic and philosophical, it might help to know that I have confronted (thankfully only temporarily) the idea of a premature death, given all of my health problems, and I have found the knowledge of my body nourishing new life to be of great comfort.

One of my favourite examples of the nourishing effects of death is western hemlock. Its seeds fall onto its own fallen branches, which release nutrients gradually as they decompose, and which its seedling can use. And its legacy doesn't simply benefit its own offspring – the rotting branches also provide food for fungi, insects, beetles and billions of micro-organisms. Eventually, as the parent tree dies, its children will take its place, having got off to a flying start.

When we see death as a part of life then we no longer need to fear it, and we have no need to invent an afterlife, a heaven or reincarnation to allow us to cope with the fact of our own mortality, and that of our loved ones. I believe that if we made a collective decision to embrace the idea of death, rather than trying to be immortal (as we do when we attempt to create genetic or technological elixirs of youth, or invent souls, essences, spirits or strange 'energies') then we could take our rightful place among our cousins in the rest of the living world, knowing that this wonderful life may be brief, but it is nonetheless marvellous.

Furthermore, by embracing death we place more value on the vibrancy and preciousness of life. In my experience the knowledge of your own mortality can be employed as a motivating factor. I know it gives me a sense of urgency to try to effect change and to make a difference before I depart.

Because we don't like talking about death, we don't like planning for it either. 'Death cafés' are a novel idea where this taboo subject is discussed openly in a supportive environment.

Furthermore, our deaths can lead to environmental damage – for example, from chemical-laden coffins, or those made by felling precious hardwood trees; and energy-intensive cremations causing toxins from coffins to be released into the atmosphere. I'm sure, if they thought about it, most people wouldn't want their death to be toxic, but because we don't plan for death, loved ones, in their grief, opt for the limited choices offered to them. There are alternatives, such as wicker or cardboard coffins, and woodland burials, and thankfully these are becoming more common. A tree planted in your loved one's memory is a poignant legacy. You can plant a tree in many woodlands and know that the tree represents new life. When you choose to be buried in a woodland you nourish new life directly.

Even when we are able to embrace this natural philosophy of death, it is inevitable that the death of a loved one will involve grief. Mourning is the price we pay for creating loving bonds with our friends and family. I am no expert, but I do know that grief and mourning cannot be suppressed without creating problems in the future. Memorial celebrations are a time for expressing that grief (which will be different for everyone), for connectedness, for feelings that we are not alone, and for remembering what made that person unique.

When we talk about the cycles of life and death we should also discuss ageing – another highly regulated area of our society. As a middle-aged woman I am strongly encouraged to dye my grey hairs instead of embracing them. Adverts and magazines tell me that I should do something about my wrinkles and my saggy

189

bits. They encourage me to have operations to modify my body. But why? I like ageing. I'm very happy with my imperfections and I have no regrets about my life, even though I have not achieved a fraction of the things I would have liked. But that's OK. Of course I get defensive when someone criticises my appearance, but it only reinforces the sad fact that so few of us have the courage to stand up and declare that it's not OK to treat older people as second class. I like to look at myself as I look at a mature tree – with every scar (internal and external) as a marker to show that I've lived. Men and women, let's shout out our maturity, experience and wisdom, loud and proud!

Trees show us that we should use the ageing process to spur us on – to up our production of flowers and fruit because time may be short. Life is exciting and we can meet new people, have new experiences, develop new ideas and plans for action. This is no time to look back – we have so much left to do.

Case study

Katie, formerly a palliative care nurse, now supports people at any time of life to plan and design the death they would like.

"A core part of my experience as a permaculture practitioner is to design for as good a quality of life for land and people as possible. However, within my work and life, I frequently observe that how we die in Britain is detrimental to our care of the Earth, each other, and how we share resources fairly.

My experience of working alongside dying people and their families is that the majority of people are pleased and relieved not only to talk about their fears around death and dying, but also to make positive plans for the kind of death they would like. My own observations of dying people, and then their bereaved relatives, is that those who have talked openly and honestly about death and dying, and have planned for what they would like to happen, tend to have a more peaceful, meaningful time at the end of their life."

Exercise

Write a 'creative dying' plan. Consider your end of life care, and your wishes for after your death. What would you like for a celebration? Consider the impact of your choices on the people around you and on other living beings.

Create conditions conducive to life

"The world has enough for everyone's need, but not everyone's greed."
Mahatma Gandhi

When parent trees send their seeds off into the world, they don't know whether their offspring will successfully germinate. Sycamores project their seeds that fly like helicopters to discover new ground. They have very little control over the offspring themselves, so instead they go to extraordinary lengths to ensure that the conditions in which their offspring will grow up will be conducive to life. They contribute to the larger ecosystem so that their offspring will grow up in a healthy, safe environment which offers protection and opportunities for resilience. As we have discovered earlier in the book, trees gather in forests that regulate temperature, water, and create fertile soil – ideal conditions for their offspring even when the parents are not around.

If we adopt a tree-like, forward-looking approach for our own children we can explore what we would want for them if we took ourselves out of the equation. For example, we would probably want them to develop strengths such as independence, self-confidence, finding their purpose in life, and the ability to create their own happiness. How can we establish the foundations so that they can thrive even when we are not around? Or help them to discover their independence even while we are? We might want to remove some of the barriers that we may be putting in the way of this progress, like being over-protective, risk-averse, unconsciously undermining their confidence, or being too pushy. Instead we can step back, let them make mistakes and discover things the 'hard way', so that they can develop the resources to overcome future difficulties. We cannot protect them from every hardship in life, such as relationship break-ups or job-losses, illness and tough times. But if we create the right conditions, we can set them up for a successful, independent life of their own.

As a society we all, collectively, have responsibility for the health of future generations. This might be in the form of providing a high-quality, well-rounded education for all, and ensuring that no child is raised in poverty, and that parents receive the support they need to deal with their own problems.

Children need emotional security. Compassion, affection, self-esteem, trust and gratitude are all developed during childhood, and, sadly, children brought up in environments of extreme stress have been shown to be more fearful of those who are different from them (for example, someone of another ethnic group or gender), and less open to new ideas.[1] Growing up in a society and in physical surroundings that nurture rather than cause damage could turn life around for millions of children and their parents, and would have knock-on benefits for all of us.

On a global scale we should support children in war zones or areas of famine, regardless of the causes, ethnicities or national boundaries. We each have a responsibility not to leave that duty to someone else – in the same way that each tree contributes in promoting growth, shelter and sharing of nutrients to benefit the whole forest. A simple way to help fulfil this responsibility is to sponsor a child in a developing country.

Those people in the developed world who have benefitted greatly from huge transfers in property and other wealth can share that prosperity to create better lives for younger generations struggling to afford a place to live.

At the other end of the age scale, creating conditions conducive to longevity include respecting and caring for our older generations, and valuing their wisdom and the continued practical contribution they can make.

Creating ideal conditions for others to thrive is a co-operative endeavour – just like the efforts of mangrove species that work together to create entirely stable coastlines (incidentally this is something that cannot be replicated successfully by man-made means). Mangroves don't hold the belief that they need to all act as individuals, as we are often encouraged to do, and that those benefitting from their efforts are freeloaders.

Additionally, we can create cultures where people feel safe to express their views, and to innovate. As individuals we can do this by acting as facilitators, creating potential bonds from which creative ideas and solutions emerge. You don't need to be in a position of great power to do this. Introducing two friends who have similar interests; joining a community group; or sharing skills or knowledge all promote fertile environments in which 'acorn' ideas can grow. In the workplace too, we can see benefits for wellbeing and productivity when we create the right conditions for innovative ideas to emerge.

Universities, learning establishments and industries have enormous potential for creating fertile environments for change – for example, in supporting innovative renewable technologies. Renewable and regenerative solutions are often underfunded, or they may even be derailed by those with vested interests in maintaining the current destructive trajectory of growth. The prevailing view is that technological, rather than nature-based, solutions are superior for solving the world's problems. Those that look solely to technological solutions are perhaps unaware that nature has solved almost every problem we are currently facing. For example, trees invented carbon capture and storage long before engineers did! Remember too, the principle we discovered in Group 2, that **each activity or element should fulfil several needs.** Carbon capture and storage has one use (carbon sequestration), whereas trees have multiple uses – including carbon sequestration, water regulation, windbreaks, habitats for people and other creatures, and are a source of sustainable timber and food. If engineers can design all that into one machine then I'll be very impressed!

There is an urgent need for disciplines such as biomimicry, permaculture and ecopsychology to be embedded at all levels of academic research and business, from psychology to design, and from engineering to agricultural research. This could happen quickly if we embrace a mind-shift about the value of the natural world. Universities and businesses are often located in urban environments, so academics are unlikely to look out of their windows and wonder how nature would solve a problem; but the bringing together of experts in multi-disciplinary teams to include biologists and ecologists (as indeed is happening in many universities) can speed up the process of development. We can see multi-disciplinary teams as forests or other 'super-organisms', sharing resources and solutions.

Turning now to governments – their role in creating conditions conducive to sustainable progress needs to start by measuring what is important. We know from many years of school league tables, and measures such as GDP (gross domestic product), that when we set a target in place people work towards it, however detrimental they believe it to be. Ditching school league tables and instituting targets for child wellbeing would help children reach their potential and be happier and healthier. Bringing in Gross National Happiness[2] measures would be a big step to benefit all of us. Personal wellbeing already exists as a measure in the UK, but little weight is placed on it[3] – in Bhutan, on the other hand, it is actively pursued by government.[4] Bringing experts and lay people into the democratic process, via methods such as Citizens' Assemblies, Citizens' Juries and Consensus Conferences can also result in practical and innovative solutions to a wide range of political, social, economic and environmental issues.[5]

On a personal level, one vital aspect of creating conditions conducive to life is to let go of the need to know that your action will be successful. A tree has no idea if even one of its seeds will reach maturity but it continues to create ideal conditions, being part of the community that shelters and nurtures a giant ecosystem. In my experience, you may have to struggle against the natural tendency to give up at the *"I'm not sure it's going to work"* or *"I'm too small to make a difference"* stage.

Creating conditions conducive to life involves a shift in your thinking from purely passive consuming to creating. Consuming without creating is a one-way process that depletes what is around you – it is an activity that values the 'now' over the future. Creating is a regenerative process, making more and more from the resources that you have. It is forward-looking, but the action taken is in the here and now, and you will experience a deep sense of fulfilment in knowing that you are creating something magical. Some simple illustrations of this psychological shift include: buying a T-shirt (consuming), learning to sew (creating); watching TV (consuming), giving practical support to the local theatre company (creating); taking your child to the play park (consuming), helping to create a school garden (creating); dropping your kids at the school gate (consuming), joining the Parent Association (creating); going to the gym (consuming), raising money via charity runs (creating); buying herbs at the supermarket (consuming), growing pots on your windowsill (creating). None of these consumer activities that I have mentioned are inherently bad (in fact they may be positively beneficial) and I'm not saying we should stop buying/consuming things we need, but the mind-shift in looking at what we consume in a different way is profound. At Whistlewood, our community woodland, we encourage this in simple ways, such as actively involving people who come for meetings or workshops in planning, setting up, making tea and clearing up at the end. Even paying customers find it a more welcoming and inclusive approach because they feel more connected to the organisation and its aims. This type of change shifts us from passive consumers to conscious and active participants in our own lives, those of our fellow beings, and those of future generations.

Learning from forests in this way leads to a sense of empowerment and confidence. Whether you aim to effect change on a grand or more modest scale, everyone has a role to play. When you feel it's right to be a 'consumer', give yourself permission, don't feel guilty – we all have needs, but consider how you can make changes moving forwards. The important thing to remember is to fertilise the ground, sow the seeds, create ideal conditions, remain active in preserving the life support system, and then allow those you have provided for to bring their talents to the fore.

Exercise

List all the activities you undertake in a week and all the categories of things you consume. This might include your activities and purchasing decisions in your personal life, your home, your community and your workplace.

For each activity and purchasing decision, decide whether it was based primarily on consumption or creation.

For those activities and decisions based mainly on consumption only, list ways you can you switch from being a consumer to a creator in this context.

Replicate and build on
strategies that work

"After 3.8 billion years of research and development, failures are fossils, and what surrounds us is the secret to survival."

Janine Benyus

What if we could solve every one of the world's problems by purely technological means – if we could live on a planet devoid of life except our own? We would still be alive (indeed we might by then be immortal), and we could put in place measures that would define our happiness and our technological solutions as 'successful'. We could invent entirely new strategies, based not on the past 3.8 billion years of success, but on technologies entirely dreamed up in the minds of twenty-first-century humans. Yet that's not a place I would want to live. I'm guessing none of us would. I would also contend that these radical technological solutions, in the absence of nature, would be unlikely to endure.

Natural systems build on strategies that already work. When trees evolved from non-woody plants, they thickened up their predecessor's already existing stems. When single-celled organisms built into complex oaks, they did so by adding cell upon cell, a strategy that had already been proven to work. Nature doesn't reinvent the wheel when it doesn't have to. (Incidentally: nature has only invented the wheel a couple of times, in bacteria. Alternative solutions, like legs and branches, fins and wings, avoid vulnerable axles and can navigate a far wider range of terrains – that's why you'll never see a mountain goat awaiting a breakdown service.)

In this principle, we will explore just a few real-life ways that human innovators have taken nature's successes, learned from them and built on them.

"I think the biggest innovations of the 21st century will be at the intersection of biology and technology. A new era is beginning."

Steve Jobs

197

Agriculture and horticulture

The UN Conference on Trade and Development concluded in 2013 that to feed the world's population and respond to climate change necessitates a transformative change in our food and agricultural systems.[1] The traditional view that organic and regenerative agriculture cannot feed the world has been overturned by studies that show these are viable alternatives.[2] Learning from nature (and taking heed of the research into existing new types of farming methods), we must diversify, increase food sovereignty (allow people to define their own food and agricultural systems) and re-localise food production, which will necessitate a move to small-scale farming.

Here are some of the agricultural and horticultural techniques that can be part of the solution.

Regenerative agriculture

Regenerative agricultural practices renew and build soil, sequester carbon, restore biodiversity and improve water management. Farmers take a holistic approach to the farm and surrounding ecosystems. These practices can include the following.

Organic agriculture
This involves growing without synthetic pesticides or fertilisers. Codes also prohibit antibiotics and growth hormones (with a few exceptions), and growers operate crop rotation for plant health. Organic practices can be used on farms, in gardens, allotments or community projects. A successful example is Yeo Valley organic dairy farm in Somerset, UK.[3] They raise dairy cows, but also grow organic feed and employ wildlife conservation methods for biodiversity and for pest control.

No-dig/no-till methods
These methods involve growing with minimal turning of the soil (a strategy overwhelmingly seen in nature). Growers add compost and manure to improve soil structure, biodiversity and fertility. A very inspiring case study is Charles Dowding's no-dig commercial market garden at Longacres, Somerset, UK, which produces £25,000 of vegetables with just 70–80 hours labour per

week.[4] Kew Gardens in London has also converted to no-dig in their kitchen gardens.

Agroforestry

This is growing crops, or raising livestock, in combination with trees or shrubs, with benefits for soil composition, surface water runoff and crop health. Agroforestry practices are used all over the world, one example of which is in southern Malawi, where maize is intercropped with fertilising trees, tripling the output of maize.[5]

Holistic management

Pioneered by Zimbabwean farmer and ecologist, Alan Savory, holistic livestock management mimics nature by rotating animals, restoring grassland (including turning deserts into fertile green farms), increasing biodiversity, and providing food security for local people.[6]

Permaculture

This is a design system for creating agricultural and social systems using a set of ethics and principles inspired by observations in nature. As a design system for growing food, it can be used for small plots (e.g. gardens and allotments), for community spaces, and for large-scale farms. Permaculture is often misunderstood as being simply organic gardening, but the design principles can be used for every aspect of life. The forest garden created by the founders of *Permaculture Magazine*, Tim and Maddy Harland, in Hampshire, UK, is an example of how a permaculture-designed plot can produce food for a family, support wildlife, and provide a garden to for children to play in.[7] Anyone can integrate permaculture into their daily lives and there are courses available around the world for people who want to learn more about it.

Community-supported agriculture (CSA)

Community-supported agriculture is a partnership between farmers and consumers, where the risks and rewards are shared, and customers have an active role in the growing of their food. There are various models of CSA, including producer-led, where customers pay a subscription in exchange for produce; and producer–community partnerships, via co-operative structures.[8] The community-led agriculture model involves communities initiating growing projects, with labour being voluntary or paid, and produce being distributed among members and sold. Or farms can be community-owned, such as Fordall Farm, an organic mixed farm in Shropshire, UK, which has over 8000 community shareholders.[9] CSAs also operate in cities – for example, Detroit's City Commons.[10]

WWOOF (World Wide Opportunities on Organic Farms)[11]
This is a scheme for anyone to gain experience volunteering on organic farms. Farmers share their knowledge and receive help on the farm in return for a bed and food.

Sustainable communities

Transition Network[12]
Originating in Totnes in Devon, UK, but now in 50 countries, each Transition town brings people together to re-imagine and rebuild the world. The aim is for communities to start locally to address some of the big issues of today, such as our environmental impact and social and economic insecurity. They aim to increase resilience to future shocks. Focusing on practical projects and supportive communities, Transition groups define their own projects based on local ideas and needs, and may focus on teaching skills, promoting or growing local food, re-localising economic systems (such as creating local currencies), promoting creative energy solutions, and re-imagining work. Transition town Totnes is a group that has projects ranging from local energy, affordable low-impact housing, local food, creating livelihoods and sharing skills.[13] In the USA, Local 20/20 in East Jefferson County, New York State, has initiated, among other projects, an Economic Localization Action Group to create a local-based resilient economy.[14] They have created a local currency, and formed the Local Investing Opportunities Network (LION), which has facilitated the investment of over $7.6 million to over 75 local businesses.

Nature-inspired design

One of nature-inspired designers' secrets to success for creating goods, services, buildings, food systems and wellbeing strategies is to fit form to function. In other words, they look for the *why?* first, and then follow up with the *what?* We might explore this in a tree – the function might include protection, stability, and transporting nutrients and water over long distances. The form is a trunk. While in trees this happened via evolutionary trial and error processes, we can do the same much more quickly – by trial and error *and* by using our innovative brains to shortcut creative processes. Starting by thinking of the uses that a product or system will have doesn't mean that it can't also be beautiful. Look at a butterfly's wings for example.

Biomimicry
The Biomimicry Institute[15] offers this definition:

"Biomimicry is an approach to innovation that seeks sustainable solutions to human challenges by emulating nature's time-tested patterns and strategies. The goal is to create products, processes, and policies—new ways of living—that are well adapted to life on earth over the long haul."

Biomimicry has applications in all walks of life, but in particular: science, innovation, architecture, design and business. Asknature.org has compiled some of nature's solutions in one place.

Designers all over the world are using nature's success stories to solve problems. Lotusan® by Sto,[16] is an exterior paint that mimics the micro-structural processes found on the surface of leaves and the wings of insects, making them resistant to dirt and able to remain clean with a simple shower of water. Colombia Forest Products has invented a formaldehyde-free plywood, based on the process employed by mussels to cling to rocks.[17]

Nature-inspired/ biomimetic architecture
Seattle's Bullitt Centre in the USA aims to be the greenest commercial building in the world, modelled on an evergreen forest.[18]

The Eastgate Centre in Harare in Zimbabwe has been constructed to be ventilated and cooled by natural means, inspired by the way termites cool their mounds.[19]

In Milan, Italy, 'vertical forests' designed by architect Stefano Boeri comprise over 20,000 m² of forests spread over the balconies of two residential tower blocks, with benefits for biodiversity, air quality, carbon sequestration, shade and noise reduction.[20]

Green building – natural materials
Architects and builders are reviving natural materials, such as straw bales, limecrete, wood and cob. In addition, new materials are being invented based on natural processes. One company, Calera, has created a cement made by a similar process to mother of pearl, which has the benefit of sequestering carbon.[21]

Nature-inspired energy systems

Solar Botanic Limited has designed artificial trees that convert solar and wind power into electricity via 'nanoleaf' electromagnetic connectors.[22] A further innovation, developed by researchers at Massachusetts Institute of Technology, is an optimal layout of solar panels for concentrated solar plants, based on the Fibonacci sequence found in sunflowers.[23]

Many nature-inspired energy solutions opt for decentralised plants, which are more resilient to political and economic shocks. There are numerous examples of community-owned renewable energy systems (solar, wind, hydro) that democratise the energy market, such as the ATDER-BL hydro projects in Nicaragua, which provide electricity and water to rural communities.[24]

Nature-inspired business and economic systems[25]

Clearly the capitalist growth economy is not working, either in social or environmental terms. A system that pulls resources away from the many (both human and non-human) for the benefit of a few people does not uphold the natural principles that we have explored in this book. Professor Tim Jackson's book *Prosperity without Growth*[26] explores the issues of growth, stating that:

"the new macro-economics will need to be ecologically and socially literate, ending the folly of separating economy from society and environment".

Jackson states that a resilient economy will still consist of the current fundamental economic variables, such as spending and saving, production of goods and services, and government revenue and spending, but they will be augmented with systems to reflect the value of natural resources – physical, social and ecosystems, and the value of ecological investment and the focus on long-term goals.

Other commentators have focused on qualitative rather than quantitative growth, noting that living systems grow, but in a sustainable way that includes expansion, decline and recycling.[27]

Circular economies
These mimic natural systems and are restorative, rely on renewable energy, create a closed loop for waste and resources, and eliminate toxic materials. A transformation to circular economies and business practices requires a switch to collaborative rather than competitive interaction. There are financial benefits too, with savings in scarce resources and increased employee satisfaction. Trillions of dollars of private green investment is already being reported.[28]

Solidarity economies
These create relationships of mutual support, localise and democratise communities, and work within a shared set of ethics based on social, economic and environmental values.

The Commons
This is a collaborative approach to holding natural or cultural resources as 'commons', for the benefit of all, as opposed to being in private ownership. Examples include the 2 billion people around the world who rely for their livelihood on common fisheries, forests, water and other natural resources. Cultural commons can include science, medical advances, innovations in genetics, literature, the internet and art.

Nature-inspired businesses and organisations
These businesses are systems-focused, collaborative, dynamic, and benefit from diversity. This has benefits for employee satisfaction, innovation and adaptability.

A non-profit example is the Dutch Buurtzog neighbourhood care system, a highly successful organisation that organises employees into small groups that plan their own administration, scheduling and patient care. Each group serves the needs of the same 50 patients.[29] In the private sector, the US company Sun Hydraulics has project teams that are entirely self-managed. The company has 900 employees and has reported profits for over 30 years, with no lay-offs.[30] A French company FAVI, which primarily makes gearbox forks, has 500 employees organised into self-organising groups. The company has good profits, high-quality products, and excellent customer satisfaction. It has, unlike its competitors, avoided outsourcing its manufacturing to China.[31]

Climate strategies

Project Drawdown (www.drawdown.org) lists the top 80 strategies for climate mitigation as researched by experts from around the world. Take a look – they might not be what you expect (for example, reducing food waste comes in at number 3, which is higher than any of the transport solutions).[32] Many of the solutions involve trees and plants:

Seven of the top 20 involve changes to agricultural practices like those listed above. At numbers 5, 12, 13 and 14 are restoration of forests and peatlands (supporting nature in its vital job of regulating the planet's climate).

Most of the solutions have additional social and health benefits such as a plant-rich diet (number 4), educating girls (number 6), family planning (number 70), clean cook-stoves (number 21), and walkable cities (number 54), proving that effort and expenditure on climate solutions will have additional dividends for everyone.

In conclusion, there are millions of examples around the world of people, businesses and projects learning from nature and applying this in a practical way. There are too many to list them here, but a quick internet search will direct you to activities in your region, wherever you are.

Exercise

Discover a nature-inspired project or company in your local area. What can you do to be part of it, support and publicise it? Most projects are very happy (if not totally overjoyed!) to welcome volunteers. What are you waiting for?

Why not share information about the ideas and projects you discover, too – particularly if you work in the media. There is not yet sufficient mainstream exposure of the amazing projects and innovative ideas being worked on around the world.

Be a good ancestor

"Look and listen for the welfare of the whole people and have always in view not only the past and present but also the coming generations, even those whose faces are yet beneath the surface of the ground – the unborn of the future nation."

Constitution of the Iroquois Nation

As we near the end of this book, you may be looking for the tree's one simple answer to the meaning of life, the universe and everything, so that you can bring that wisdom into your own life. Massive drum-roll ... here it is:

Be a good ancestor.

That's it – it's incredibly simple! (Yeah, OK I'll admit we've not found it simple so far, but let's make a start now.)

So how does nature approach being a good ancestor? The main aim in life of all living things is to pass on packets of wondrously complex information encoded in their DNA, and have that information continue on, with modifications, through as many generations as possible. That purpose, which all living things share, creates everything we have around us in the natural world – the soil, the forests, grasslands and ocean life; creatures in the sky, the seas and in millions of adaptive niches. The ancestors of the beings alive today have created colours throughout the spectrum, many that we can't even see; shapes and sizes to fit all purposes; textures ranging from silky soft to rough and leathery. Nature creates rain, wind and frost, and captures yet protects against sunlight. DNA codes for love and joy, empathy and connectedness, protection and co-operation. It creates wings, fins, proboscises, ears, roots and trunks (trees' and elephants'), and hundreds of thousands of adaptations whose functions we haven't yet discovered. Living things can make materials stronger than any we can create; use protective mechanisms to keep even the most persistent invader at bay; and have body shapes that fly non-stop around the world.

And our ancestors have created beauty – beauty for our eyes and ears and touch, in the form of the shape and colour of butterflies, in the smell of a rose, the faces of our children, and the touch of our lover. For me, when I contemplate the bigger

206

questions of why we are here, I have no need to find any more meaning than that.

Trees show us that the strongest purpose we can have is to make an effort throughout our lives to be the best ancestor we can be. To do that we must recognise that the way we live has the potential to deprive our descendents of positive futures for themselves, or alternatively our decisions, as individuals and collectively, can create a better future for us and our descendants.

One way to start is to actively seek happiness, calm and inner peace by finding the sweet spot – the place where you have 'enough'. Our tree cousins tell us that **'enough' is what we should strive for**, and that appreciating when we have enough will be beneficial for ourselves and our descendents. The opposite of scarcity isn't having everything you want. It is about having everything you need – material, emotional and psychological – *and* knowing that is abundance in itself. We can choose gratitude for what we have, rather than feeling that we never have enough and are therefore never good enough. If 'having enough-ism' became the prevailing world philosophy, then each individual whose basic needs are met could embrace the happiness of being who they are, where they are, and content with what they have. Those who have more could use their mycorrhizal networks to share with those who are not yet there. The amazing thing is that each and every one of us can declare that as our aim today. Throughout this book, I hope that you have discovered many strategies for living more successfully and with improved wellbeing. I hope that you can keep them with you on a daily basis to guide you on your journey as I do. These principles can be used for all sorts of decision-making. But is there also a shortcut to help us to make the right choices when we are faced with hundreds, even thousands, each day? Our lives are so complex that decisions that would have been easy 100 years ago (*"I'll buy what the local shopkeeper stocks"* or *"I'll eat what is growing in my garden "*) are turned into minefields (*"Which of the hundreds of different products on the supermarket shelves should I choose to keep my whole family happy? "*). Whatever we do we seem to get it wrong, and feel guilty about it – a double whammy. There is one relatively simple solution that I've discovered to guide you in making the right decisions, which is to ask yourself *"**will that choice make me a good ancestor?**"*

207

This idea is not new. The Native American concept of seven-generational thinking imposes a duty to consider the impact of every decision on the seventh generation into the future. That equates to roughly 150–200 years. To do that we don't need a crystal ball, but we do need to deliberate on each decision and decide whether it is likely to have the outcome of creating more abundance, or of destroying it. When we seek to apportion responsibility for the mess we are now in, we know that it was created not just by the decisions taken today or yesterday but those taken by our ancestors 200 years ago. There is no point right now in blaming them (or worse, using that to absolve ourselves of responsibility), but we should ask ourselves – do we want to inflict that lack of forethought on future generations?

There are hundreds of easy decisions to be made by following this simple thought process. Should I buy that plastic novelty toy? No, that won't make me a good ancestor. Should I buy a pair of trousers that I'm going to only wear once? No. Should I fly when I could easily take the train? No. Should I buy a dining table made from illegally logged rainforest timber? No. Should I switch to electricity from renewable sources? Yes. Should I do some community volunteering work? Yes. Should I take my reusable cup to the coffee shop? Yes. Should I keep my phone rather than upgrading it each year? Yes. Should I use toiletries and cleaning products that don't pollute the land or water? Yes. Should I invest my savings or pension ethically? Yes. Should I plant some trees? Yes yes yes! There is a saying *"it's not easy being green"* but it is remarkable how many decisions become *really easy* when you ask yourself the ancestor question.

But of course there are some decisions that are harder. Should I buy organic food from Kenya or local non-organic food? Should I buy leather shoes as a by-product of the meat industry or vegan shoes made from plastic? Should I buy meat from my local organic, ethical butcher or be vegetarian? Should I read my children a bedtime story or go and visit my grandma in her nursing home? Should I buy clothes from abroad if the profits go to help local communities? Often there are no easy answers, but you can do some research and give it some thought and then ask yourself the ancestor question again.[1]

Seven-generational thinking urges us not to say *"It's too difficult to decide, I'll take the easy option"*. Try to make the best decision you can at the time. Your answers will be different from mine, depending on your budget, your health, support networks, time and commitments. Despite my ethical ideals I do have to make some very strange choices because of my health (like buying asparagus all year round, because it's one of just a handful of fruit and vegetables I'm not allergic to), but I try to balance them with other things that are easier for me (like buying clothes from vintage shops rather than buying new, and making the decision, as I did recently, to travel from Derbyshire to the south of France by train rather than by plane.

Start with your own 'easy wins' first then build on them. That way you are less likely to become demoralised. Your changes might be in the categories of food, transport, purchasing decisions, conservation, investments, or energy consumption, for example.

When you are making decisions (or maybe avoiding them) beware the psychological traps waiting for you – calling you like honey tempts Winnie the Pooh. (It's at this point in the book I realise that I have far too few literary references and far too many from children's stories!) Here are some of the gremlins that will pop up to try and outweigh the ancestor question, and some potential ways you might tackle those pesky thoughts:

– *"I haven't got time."* You might ask yourself if you really don't have time, or if you are just choosing to spend your time in a different way. Millions of people from all walks of life are already finding time.

– *"It's too expensive."* Can you shift your buying choices? Many of the decisions involve saving money (the best of which is not buying stuff you don't need). Instead of asking yourself why something is so expensive (like organic food, formerly known as 'food'), you might ask why chemically grown food is so cheap.

– *"That green technology isn't perfect."* Be an early adopter to create markets for green companies, and provide feedback to help them improve their products. Solar panels and electric cars have improved and prices have come down, even though there is still progress to be made.

- *"Being green is for the middle classes. Poor people can't afford to do that."* Do what you can. If you can afford it, or can shift your priorities, then do it. Too many people use others as an excuse not to make an effort.
- *"If we stop buying stuff everyone will be out of a job."* But if we don't stop buying stuff everyone might be out of a habitable planet! Greener solutions create jobs too – the best systems don't design out the role of people in the creation of wealth on the planet. Companies, economies and systems will adapt, and are already doing so.
- *"My actions are too small to make a difference."* More on this in the next principle.
- *"I'll leave it to governments or companies to make my choices."* Seriously?!!! I think we've waited long enough. (Incidentally, if you are politician, company executive or other person in a position of influence, please pull your finger out.)[2]

The most effective ways to tackle these gremlins is to tap into the emotional aspects of why you want to make the right choices, why you want to live a better life, and to imagine the positive wellbeing when you find your purpose and contribute to a healthier world. Find your motivation in whichever way works for you, and surround yourself with other people who are future-looking.

Our throwaway consumer society encourages us always to go for the cheapest option – the one that will soon break so we have to buy a new one (it's called 'planned obsolescence' and is a deliberate tactic of companies to make goods with a limited lifespan). When faced with buying decisions, I try to remember that if the true costs of goods and services (like pollution, environmental costs, cheap wages, resource depletion and waste) were included in their price, many of the cheap alternatives would be much more expensive or *would not even exist.*

Take air travel for example. If the true cost of carbon emission, environmental damage, and harm to local wildlife (for example, of holiday complexes on beaches) were taken into account in the price of a holiday, then choosing whether to fly or go by train would be financially really easy. If governments didn't subsidise fossil fuels, then renewable electricity would be cheaper by a long way (although it already is in some cases). Next time you choose between a cheaper and a more expensive option, ask yourself what the true costs might be in environmental and social terms, and allow your decision to be guided by that knowledge.

Another ancestor question to ask ourselves is which ethical responsibilities are we outsourcing to someone else? We outsource all kinds of ethical responsibilities. Not all of them are detrimental – we do it as a welcome way to simplify our lives and bring in expertise. For example, most of us make the decision to send our children to school, and trust teachers to give them the best education. However, we will get pretty instant feedback – if our child comes home crying every day, we will quickly go to school and find out what's wrong. More and more older people are living in nursing homes, and we trust staff to look after them, but if we don't visit how will we know that they are being cared for properly? The feedback mechanisms break down if we look away.

Most of us outsource the ethical consequences of our purchases – from food, to clothes, to appliances. It's more comfortable[3] and easier not to have to think about the low wages, the deforestation, and the huge carbon costs that may have been incurred in getting them to our stores. In fact it's often difficult to even raise these issues, so much do we hate feeling guilty and making others feel guilty. (As an aside: making other people feel ashamed doesn't work as a tactic to motivate change anyway.)

However, many of the feedback mechanisms that might regulate behaviour have only broken down relatively recently. Five hundred years ago (or even in my childhood, growing up in a Leicestershire village), if I walked past a farmer's field and saw him mistreating his pigs, I would tell my neighbours and they would come together to have a word with the farmer, or would have made the decision to buy their pork elsewhere. He would very probably have changed his behaviour or gone out of business. Because we no longer see into the pig sty (or can choose not to) then we hand over control to industrial factory farms, with our dinner arriving in a sanitised plastic wrapper. When we buy some biscuits, an orangutan doesn't turn up dead on our table because our palm oil has destroyed its home; and when we buy a mobile phone, a miner doesn't rock up for tea,

211

angry at us for poisoning him and his family via toxic minerals they have been exposed to. Of course things weren't always rosy in the past, but until the industrial revolution we mainly had to look the consequences of our choices in the face, and decide head-on whether to continue making them. It was more difficult to look away.

If you are up for the challenge, consider mentally conducting an outsourcing audit. On a piece of paper, list all your activities and purchasing habits and then examine what emotions (not just thoughts) arise when you look at each one. Some habits you will be able to change with only a little effort (ditch the palm oil for the benefit of the orangutans), and others will be harder. Because of that, you may also decide that a simpler life is easier than trying to find ethical alternatives to things that don't actually matter (like non-essential clothing), and some purchases can't be justified at all (such as single-use plastic). It's not easy but you can try to bring as much ethical responsibility back in-house as you can, and outsource only those decisions whose consequences are visible and acceptable to you. But the number-one rule is don't get paralysed by guilt in the process – that will do no-one any good, least of all you.

While our emotions often encourage us to look away, we are not immune to the suffering in the world. We spend an enormous amount of energy suppressing guilt and pain, justifying the indefensible, denying realities and making excuses. I believe this is causing us harm as individuals, both mentally and physically. When we block out the bad things, the good things get pushed down too, and we become less able to experience joy, calm, peace, beauty and happiness. It takes courage to reconnect with the feelings that we are told are 'negative', and to turn them into positive action.

It may be that you find the idea of an 'ancestor journey' scary. Remember you are not striving for perfection, so you do not have to reach impossible heights in order to 'succeed'. There is little room for guilt, shame or feelings that you are a failure along the way. And you may find that those closest to you are not yet ready to embark on the same journey at the same time. But this is about doing what you can.

The quest story is in you, and your inner superhero is needed more than ever right now. Your challenge is to make the decision to move from the prologue of your own hero(ine)'s journey into Act One, where the action begins. You are more resilient than you think, you are not alone, and as philosopher Friedrich Nietzsche said:

"If you have a why, you can withstand almost any how."

The rewards are the stuff of legends – for you to become immortalised as the best ancestor you could possibly be.

Case study

I can certainly identify with some of the feelings that Jack had the honesty to share with me.

"I first started to care about environmental issues when I was a teenager. At that time it was the ozone layer and saving the whales, now it's climate change and plastic pollution, among other things. I joined various campaigning organisations over the years, always recycled and composted, but became depressed about the enormity of the problem and 'dropped out' because I couldn't cope with thinking about everything that was wrong with the world. I started resenting everyone around me for not doing enough. I was angry with climate deniers but read an article one day which said that environmental catastrophisers come from the same place of inaction. It made for uncomfortable reading!

Around the same time I became aware of the student strikes for climate. The teenagers that I saw on the news were me when I was their age, except now, things are even more urgent. Listening to their stories, they are using their anger and pain to spur themselves (and others) into action. Inspired by them, I decided to turn my feelings of guilt, and my excuses into doing something.

I don't have children so I'm not doing it for them. Rather selfishly, I'm doing it for me, because it's the right thing to do and I know I will feel better doing something rather than doing nothing.

I've decided to go for what's easiest for me – changing my diet, holidaying closer to home, insulating my house, and walking more rather than taking the car. I'm catching the bug, and have joined some online forums about plastic waste. I realise now that there are loads of people out there doing stuff – why hadn't I found them before?!"

Exercise

Write the script for a television programme made about you by your decendants in 200 years' time (like the *Who Do You Think You Are?* TV show).

What would they discover about you? Would they be proud?

This exercise may be painful and raise lots of different emotions. If uncomfortable feelings come to the fore, then don't shy away, but use them to spur yourself into action.

If you're not happy with your script, write your ideal one and put in place actions to bring it into being.

Know that your actions can change the world

"The ones who are crazy enough to think that they can change the world are the ones who do."

Steve Jobs

Whenever I think that my modest contribution in life can't possibly make a difference, I remember the first bacterium that inhabited the Earth. That individual dot can be viewed as a tiny knot of atoms, or as the start of all life. The descendants of this miniscule creature are you, and me, and trees, and frogs, and lions, and carrots. Since that first bacterium, every single living thing has had an impact on its surroundings and has thereby helped to gradually build our whole world ecosystem.

Because none of the trillions of non-human organisms that have ever lived had the capability of thinking that they were insignificant, they have always acted as if each of them – whether beetle, cabbage, dinosaur or baobab – was the best thing ever! They have supreme confidence in their ability to survive, to grow and to effect change. I find it ironic, therefore, that as individual human beings we often think we are powerless. Yet a tiny mosquito has the power to unsettle a herd of elephants, to paraphrase an old saying.

Some people believe that everything is predestined, so nothing they do can make any difference. I don't agree. Steven Hawking expressed this perfectly when he said:

"I have noticed even people who claim everything is predestined, and that we can do nothing to change it, look before they cross the road."

To stretch this to a tree analogy, I would suggest that even the most ardent fatalist would step out of the way if a tree was falling towards them.

Every single tree that has ever lived has altered the climate, the soil and its surroundings. Every single one! So you can harness, as a source of energy and strength, the knowledge that a bacterium, mosquito or tree *can* make a difference.

215

Many people have thought about the psychological factors surrounding our relationships with the natural world. In my view, many of humanity's problems in this regard arise from an extreme *lack* of confidence, rather than an excess. Like the bully in the playground we, collectively, have deep-seated issues of insecurity that make us want to control, dominate, and express our superiority. Yet at the same time we feel shame that we have been given a great gift, as beings with consciousness, but have abused that unique role. I'm hearing more and more people refer to humans as parasites, which I find incredibly sad. But each person who calls humans a parasite is by implication calling their child, their neighbour and their friend a parasite too. To cope with any feelings of self-loathing, guilt or anger towards others, we numb the pain, and with it we numb all the positive feelings that we could be experiencing, as part of a unique and wonderful living planet – it's an emotional nightmare.

Psychology studies about human relationships may offer some insight, and some hope. They show that what differentiates people who have a sense of love and belonging from those who feel shame and the belief that they are not good enough, is that the first group feel that they are *worthy of belonging*.[1] That is the separating factor. So the implication is that if we can cultivate that feeling that we are worthy of living on planet Earth, we will reap the rewards in terms of mutual support, love, connection, and a confidence that we have a valuable role to play. Until we are compassionate with ourselves we cannot be compassionate with other beings, whether human or otherwise. To achieve this we must have the courage to embrace the vulnerability that giving up control brings, and we must be comfortable with our own imperfections as individuals and as a species. Fortunately, if we open our eyes, we can see other species modelling this behaviour right across the spectrum – they are imperfect and vulnerable and yet we know that they belong here.

So, having put forward the argument that all of us belong on this planet, and that every one of us plays a contributory role, what next? Primatologist and anthropologist, Jane Goodall said:

"You cannot get through a single day without having an impact on the world around you. What you do makes a difference, and you have to decide what kind of difference you want to make."

Often we look at changing the world in terms of what we are *against*. That may be racism, war, pollution, consumerism, environmental destruction or illness. But it is far more helpful to discover what you are *for*, rather than what you are against. That might be diversity, peace, a clean environment, and wellbeing for all. They may seem like two sides of the same coin, but creating a future rather than overturning a past is how nature approaches things. If you feed what you are *for* with good compost, water and sunlight, then it has an excellent chance of bearing fruit, whereas if you spend all your time fighting what you are *against* (for example, weeds and pests) you might lose sight of the fact that your whole purpose was to grow fruit in the first place.

We must let go of the need to know what the results of our actions will be. The sandbox tree in Costa Rica explosively releases its seeds, and sends them spinning away at over 70 metres per second, to land some 45 metres away. The sandbox puts an enormous amount of effort into this event, but has no idea which of the seeds will root, if any. Political activist Gloria Steinman's quote seems particularly pertinent:

"The truth is that we can't know which act in the present will make the most difference in the future, but we can behave as if everything we do matters."

An impact may come through a great individual sacrifice, as for Rosa Parks, who made a decision one day to stand up for her rights, having no idea that her action would change the course of history. Or more likely, your impact will fly under the radar, every day, unrecognised except by you. Don't leave the action to someone else – ask yourself:

"If not me, then who? If not now, then when?"

Your actions do not need to be grandiose – passing on a smile, collective moments of joy in sport or music, sharing time with friends. If you have a musical talent, share it. If you can tell engaging stories, find a willing audience. When we watch the news we often see only bad things, but if we created the news according to the real balance of activities in our lives, it would be

217

filled with everyday stories of people checking on the welfare of their neighbours; parents reading their children bedtime stories; friends providing shoulders to cry on; groups restoring ecosystems; councils investing in mental health and homeless services; companies supporting new green technologies; communities planting trees; professionals dedicating their lives to the care of others; and strangers on the street helping those in need. We are social beings. We feel good when we do positive stuff. And we will go to great lengths, and make great sacrifices, to help others with no other reward than the dopamine hit that makes us feel good about ourselves, and seeing the benefits for others.

In our society where crying is a taboo, we nevertheless sit watching online videos of a man rescuing kittens from a drain, or a child experiencing elation at being able to hear for the first time. This morning I cried while watching a video about a horse being taken into a hospital (yes, a horse), to make a connection with people with terminal illnesses. I cried for three reasons simultaneously – with empathy for the man in the hospital bed; for the joy of the connection between the man and the horse; and at the courage of the hospital director who instigated such a programme. We are naturally emotional and empathetic, however hard we try (or are encouraged) to divorce ourselves from connection in the world.[2]

We are often told we are all selfish, but we donate money in our living rooms when we see a father reunited with his daughter after civil war (*BBC Comic Relief 2014* – I dare you to watch without being moved to tears). We cry at Olympic opening ceremonies when we see the world unite with one common purpose (yes, Dad, I'm talking about you), and we secretly glow with pride when our child helps a stranger or spends their evenings baking cakes for a charity sale. We forget that we are all feeling the same emotions of compassion, empathy and caring, shut in our own worlds. It's sad that many of our most emotional 'collective experiences' occur when we are alone watching TV or surfing the internet.

But might this all be a source of inspiration? If we can bring these emotions out into the open, we can see that we are not all destructive, selfish and greedy individuals, but ones who are united by the common feelings of compassion, belonging and empathy. I agree with psychologist Dr Brené Brown when she said that *"Crying with strangers in person could save the world"*.[3]

The living world teaches us that millions of small changes add up to great big, long-lasting ones. When we make changes as an individual, we create new habits. Because humans are social animals we copy each other's habits – so to live consciously, we need to become aware of who we are unconsciously copying. It may well be the neighbour up the road with the excessively large car, rather than the older person who spends their spare time volunteering at a food bank. Look at yourself as a role model too, and embrace the fact that you are an imperfect one. It is unlikely that anyone will ever give you credit for influencing or inspiring them (we are culturally terrible at giving compliments) but I promise you will be making a difference, even if you don't know it.

When many people have similar habits we create cultures. Remember that 'super-organisms' like forests, beehives or ants nests are self-organising, so the individuals within them don't wait to be told what to do. Each plays their role, brings their own talents, and together they build something they could never possibly achieve alone.

Once we have created cultures it takes much less energy input to maintain them – just as a tree in a forest uses less energy to grow upright than an individual tree standing strong against the wind. The creation of new cultures accelerates when tipping points are reached, beyond which there is a critical mass of action or outcome. In the living world we see tipping points in soil stabilisation, or tree health, for example. Human cultural examples include the demonstrations against the Vietnam war leading to its inevitable end, or more recently when the BBC TV programme *Blue Planet II* led to massive action on plastic waste. Behind both there were people who had been plugging away for years.

We saw in the *Slow and small solutions* principle, that when you put in the groundwork, change can happen rapidly – an example of which is when trees burst into leaf. If an alien arrived from space, having never seen a tree, it would be startled to see it transform from bare twigs into a green canopy in a matter of weeks (sometimes days). The small actions that you build up over time can lead to a massive blossoming of new ideas and new ways of living, perhaps when you least expect it.

The challenge for us, in our endeavours, is to be ahead of the curve, holding our nerve and trusting that the tipping point or runaway positive action will come.

At this time when there is such an urgency to effect change, when our climate and our species-loss are hurtling towards devastating tipping points in the wrong direction, there has never been more need to take action to turn those accelerations around. Ask yourself, is creating a better living world on your bucket list? If the answer is '*not yet*', what steps do you need to take, what skills do you need to gain, what confidence do you need to develop, what connections do you need to make, in order to have it as a core purpose in your life?

Environmentalist May East talks about how each day she gets up and spends some time making a conscious decision where to direct her attention that day, and therefore where she will spend her energy.[3] Whether it be activism, growing food, volunteering, planting trees or petitioning your local politician, you have a conscious decision to make about how you spend your time, with the knowledge that with each person that opts in we are closer and closer to positive change. Remember those early bacteria – if they can make a difference, you certainly can.

Exercise

What steps can you take to gain the confidence to change the world? How can you become comfortable letting go of the need to know how things will turn out? How can you join with others to create new habits, cultures and tipping points?

Love life!

"Spring is nature's way of saying 'let's party!'"

Robin Williams

When I started to recover from my illness and could spend more time out of bed, a strange thing happened. Whenever I set foot outdoors I had a feeling of exhilaration and the irresistible urge to shout at the top of my voice *"I love life!"*. Being a reserved Brit I tried to rein it in, but the urge kept coming. Sometimes I would stand in the middle of the woods and proclaim it out loud, other times it would stay as a glow of warmth inside of me. I suppose that those feelings surfaced when I discovered how incredibly fortunate I am to be alive, and therefore how much I appreciate my own life.

However, I then started pondering – why did the urge principally arise when I was outdoors? Perhaps what I was actually manifesting was my love of *all* life. Not just my own, but of all those around me: huge or miniscule; green or brown or yellow; crawling, flying, swimming or swaying in the breeze. The very fact of life is totally marvellous! Maybe that's what made me want to shout out loud and jump in the air.

Once we love someone or something in our life then it's easy to find the motivation to care for them. We can explore this idea by thinking about our motivations for looking after our children. Looking after children is hard work. It takes effort. But we don't look after our kids because of the bad things that might happen to us if we don't (like prosecution for child neglect, or that they might not look after us in our old age, or because other people will make us feel guilty if we put them out on the street). Even if we did, that wouldn't result in happy and healthy children. We make the effort to care for our kids because we love them.

The traditional way of thinking about the environment has been to consider the harm that we will do to ourselves as the primary motivator for changing our behaviour, whether the damage to us be through climate change, resource depletion or wildlife destruction. This scenario, as set out by author Charles Eisenstein, illustrates a new way of looking at the issues.[1] If we engage with all living things, not because of what they can

221

provide for us, but because we love them as beings, it is not then hard to care for them, indeed it's difficult not to, just as we love and care for our children and our other close relatives.

While many traditional environmental campaigns have focused on harm, often the most successful have been those centred around love for a place. The campaigns at the Dakota tribal area in the USA threatened by an oil pipeline, and in Sheffield in the UK where trees were threatened by the local council, are just two examples.

We can ask ourselves which spaces local to us do we love and are worth actively preserving? For which of life's riches are we willing to put in the effort needed to make a difference? Reconnect with the part of you that is still a child climbing trees, or marvelling at bugs, or scouring rock pools for crabs. In other words find that moment when you fell in love with nature.

What if we saw *life* as a fantastic party that we previously didn't realise we were invited to? Instead of being Darth Vader in *Star Wars*, aiming a ray of destruction from the Death Star towards our Earth, we could be Luke Skywalker or Princess Leia, partying with the Ewoks and the diverse species high up in the trees on a lush and verdant planet teeming with life. We might even find the happy balance between droids, people, plants, and non-human animals (we can't leave out R2D2 and C3P0, since we are unlikely to continue our evolution without some technological beings). The amazing thing is that during their struggles, Luke lost a hand, Leia commanded a fleet losing numerous pilots, and they both lost their father – but this is a moment of extreme happiness and fulfilment. They knew that their hero(ine)'s journey (their 'purpose') was to restore order to the galaxy – it was a task that they didn't know would succeed, but they did it anyway. They were willing to invest in the future. By contrast, our task of living consciously and making just one planet a better place doesn't seem so hard after all, does it?

Once we've decided that having big celebrations with the whole of the living world is what we desire, we might ponder what each party might look like – they would all be unique! There would be carnivals (partying with brightly coloured flowers perhaps), sedate tea parties (with ancient yews), illegal raves (with the riotous plants and animals at the forest edge), children's birthday parties (among acorns' sprouting shoots making their way into the world), funerals (lying peacefully with the old oaks who have passed), stuffy dinner parties (standing chatting with rows of pines), and huge weddings (joining in the celebration with the whole of the forest). The incredible thing is that nature always seems to bring more to the party than is required – it seems that butterflies are more colourful than they need to be, birds sing more beautifully, and trees put more scent in their blossom – I think that tells us that we should do the same. During these magnificent celebrations, each party-goer contributes something. The trees and plants will bring the food and provide the venue, and we can add the decorations, the entertainment and make sure the needs of each invitee, of whatever species – plant, animal or human – are well catered for. We will all show up wanting to join in the fun, share what we can, and feel the warmth of the connectedness with other beings.

It seems appropriate to end the book by willing into being these celebrations, which we can share with all the plant and animal relations we've perhaps only just realised we have. These parties can go on, whatever the future holds, however fearful we feel, or however optimistic. Whether you are young or old, whatever your race, religion, nationality, political persuasion, gender or sexuality, whether you are disabled or able-bodied – you will find your evolutionary cousins in the diversity of the forest. If we can shift our thinking, and despite the many hundreds of millions of generations that separate us, we can discover that the things we have in common will unite and guide us all. Above all, we can all celebrate in sharing this wonderful blue–green planet.

So the next time you walk in the woods, don't just hug that tree and walk on. Show your appreciation – bring your friends and let them know how off-the-scale happy you feel to belong to this great big party of life.

Think like a Tree

224

Closing words

"To really live life is to live without fear of taking the next step."
Unknown

When I was travelling in Thailand as a student I had the above saying engraved in Thai characters on a necklace that I have kept ever since. I bring it out whenever I am at a crossroads in my life and need a little extra courage to take a new direction. For all I know, the engraver may have written *"This woman is a gullible tourist "*, but if that's the case it has not lessened the power of the necklace for me and my life.

My aim in writing this book has been to bring the wisdom of the natural world to a wider audience and to explore how we can see ourselves and our lives in a different way. The systems and ways of living that are damaging the modern world were made – and therefore can be un-made – by us, working individually and together. I believe that, in the process, we will all be happier for uniting with that common purpose. Therefore, I hope that the ideas contained here have given you confidence to 'use your edge' in order to move outside of your comfort zone and to take your next step, whatever you decide that might be.

The ideas and inspiration to make our world a better place, contained in this book, have been harvested from passionate and dedicated people around the world, who have themselves persevered, overcoming barriers and setbacks. They have had the courage to envisage the world how it could be, rather than becoming discouraged by the status quo. At last the world is beginning to change and, as I write, young people around the globe are striking and protesting, imploring older generations to turn things around in order to allow them, and all of us, to have a positive future. We can be inspired and motivated both by the young activists and by the advocates for the living world who have worked for decades, campaigning and living their lives as if the future matters. Because it does.

There has never been a more important time to be active, to wake up and 'smell the pollution', but most of all to see that you, as an individual and when connecting with others, have the skills, the knowledge and the means to transform the way we all live. To transform the ways we see ourselves and others, the ways we find purpose, the ways we connect, how we can become more resilient, and to see that our happiness as individuals is inextricably linked to the way we look at the living world. By doing so we transform the now and the future simultaneously. I hope that this book has inspired you to take action to become a regeneratist, and to think like a tree.

Ten everyday ways you can live like a tree

1. **Experience nature** every day, breathe the air.
2. **Actively observe** the patterns and principles around you.
3 **Slow down** – remember to pause.
4. **Exercise your purpose** – think about your core values and where you are heading.
5. **Care for your body and mind** with good food, exercise, healing and rest; nourish your mind.
6. **Improve your surroundings** – your home, your lifestyle, your community and your world.
7. **Nurture your relationships** – develop co-operation.
8. **Do something** outside of your comfort zone.
9. **Embrace change**, celebrate failure.
10. **Make today's decisions** 'good ancestor' decisions.

The 100% in-nature challenge

Aim: to engage with the rest of the living world 100% of the time.

Here are some ideas:

1. Walk in a park or woodland.
2. Plant a pot or a window box with flowers.
3. Ask your boss to turn a disused space into a garden.
4. Share an allotment or join a community garden.
5. Cover your walls with paintings and photos of nature (cheating a bit, but this might get you the final few percent).
6. Wear flowery shirts and clothing (go on, you know you want to!).
7. Have a pot plant in your office or bedroom (that covers the question of what to do when you are asleep).
8. Do some guerrilla gardening (planting secretly in disused public spaces).
9. Take a scenic walk to work or to the shops.
10. Plant a small woodland garden in your back yard or in your local community.

Don't just plant one tree, give it a friend!

Please join in the conversation and share your experiences of using the principles and doing the challenges with your friends and on social media.

#thinklikeatree
#3naturethings
#100%innature

www.thinklikeatree.co.uk
Facebook: thinklikeatree
Instagram: thinklikeatree
Twitter: thinklikeatree5

If you've enjoyed this book, you might also like

Think like a Tree courses

Discover your potential at a range of beautiful woodland locations.

Learn how to design your life using the natural principles.

The natural principle design cycle can be used for:
- wellbeing
- health
- happiness
- confidence
- leisure
- work/livelihood
- relationships
- business
- communities
- and much more!

Think like a Tree facilitator courses

Learn how to lead your own *Think like a Tree* courses and workshops. Discover how to incorporate *Think like a Tree* into your existing practice, e.g. wellbeing, health, mental health, psychology, business management, education, working with children, vulnerable groups etc.

Think like a Tree online courses

Learn more about the natural principles, including additional tools and methods to incorporate the principles into your own life.

See **www.thinklikeatree.co.uk** for more information.

Whistlewood Common, Melbourne, Derbyshire, UK

Whistlewood is a community-owned woodland created from scratch by extra-ordinary people.

A wide range of workshops, events and activities for adults and children on:
* wellbeing
* health
* sustainable living
* forest school
* outdoor learning
* growing and cooking food
* creating resilient people and communities.

Hire of the straw-bale roundhouse for parties, workshops, corporate away-days, meetings.

Overnight camping in a beautiful yurt.

Green weddings.

You can also become a Whistlewood member to support this amazing social enterprise.

See **www.whistlewoodcommon.org** for more information.

Celebrating – with thanks

Thank you to

Gina Walker, for her patience, scientific knowledge, copious amounts of advice and editing time, and fitting the book into her incredibly busy schedule.

Eva Elliott Spencer, for her artistic talent and for spending long hours on the beautiful illustrations for the book cover and for each chapter.

Keir, for exceptional I.T. advice..

Finn, for being the best book salesman to his teachers and everyone he encounters.

Ros and Ted for endless support and for having taken the leap, fifteen years ago, to buy a beautiful smallholding and live with a somewhat mad family.

To my many wonderful friends who pulled me through some dark times over the years and have always been there when I needed them. You know who you are.

To all the 'Whistlewooders' who have given me hope and inspiration, motivation and practical support, and have endlessly demonstrated that communities are so much more important than acting as individuals.

Thanks to all the numerous course participants, friends and permaculture/nature/biomimicry colleagues who have shared resources, provided inspiration, encouragement and knowledge, and have helped hone and trial new ideas.

To The National Forest Company for encouragement and practical support with this book and the *Think like a Tree* courses. And for financial and practical support in creating our own woodland and Whistlewood.

I am grateful to everyone who has provided case studies – thank you for sharing your experiences for the benefit of others.

Finally, to Roger for putting up with me going on about 'that bloody book', and for unending love and support over the last 3 decades, especially when I've been ill and very difficult to live with. Thank you for always believing in me.

Notes

Books about trees

Some of the information about the talents of trees may seem implausible, but scientists have discovered that plants have many amazing abilities. New discoveries are being made month by month in this exciting field.

I discovered many of the facts that are contained in this book by devouring the following fascinating texts:

Tudge, Colin (2006) *The Secret Life of Trees: How They Live and Why They Matter.* Penguin Press Science.
Wohlleben, Peter (2017) *The Hidden Life of Trees: What They Feel, How They Communicate.* William Collins.
Chamovitz, Daniel (2017) *What a Plant Knows: A Field Guide to the Senses.* Updated and expanded edition. Macmillan, USA.
Adams, Max (2018) *The Wisdom of Trees: A Miscellany.* Head of Zeus.
Drori, Jonathan (2018) *Around the World in 80 Trees.* Laurence King.

About this book

1. IPCC, [Masson-Delmotte, V., P. Zhai, H.-O. Pörtner, D. Roberts, J. Skea, P.R. Shukla, A. Pirani, Moufouma-Okia, C. Péan, R. Pidcock, S. Connors, J.B.R. Matthews, Y. Chen, X. Zhou, M.I. Gomis, E. Lonnoy, Maycock, M. Tignor, and T. Waterfield (eds.)]. (2018): 'Global Warming of 1.5°C. An IPCC Special Report on the impacts of global warming of 1.5°C above pre-industrial levels and related global greenhouse gas emission pathways, in the context of strengthening the global response to the threat of climate change, sustainable development, and efforts to eradicate poverty' *World Meteorological Organization,* Geneva, Switzerland, 32 pp. See: www.ipcc.ch/sr15/

Preface

1. The National Forest covers 200 square miles of Derbyshire, Leicestershire and Staffordshire, and aims to link the two ancient Forests of Charnwood and Needwood. With a history of coalmining and heavy industry, the landscape is now that of rolling farmland, ancient forests and new planted woodlands. https://www.nationalforest.org/

2. Forest school is an outdoor education delivery model for children and young adults, that focuses on practical and personal skills, self-esteem building and independence. The concept originated in Denmark but has since been brought to many countries, including the UK, where it is integrated into many schools, supported by local councils.

3. Permaculture is a design process. It helps design intelligent systems which meet human needs while enhancing biodiversity, reducing our impact on the planet, and creating a fairer world for us all. Permaculture can involve agriculture, designing individual environments, communities, livelihoods and lives.

4. The Diploma in Applied Permaculture Design involves completing ten individual permaculture designs. See: https://www.permaculture.org.uk

5. Whistlewood is a Community Benefit Society (a type of co-operative) owned by individuals, groups and companies, who hold withdrawable shares. For more information see: www.whistlewoodcommon.org

Part 1 Woodland wisdom

1. Chamovitz, Daniel (2017) What a Plant Knows: A Field Guide to the Senses. Updated and expanded edition. Macmillan, USA.

2. Zlinszky, A., Molnár, B. and Barfod, A.S. (2017) 'Not all trees sleep the same: high temporal resolution terrestrial laser scanning shows differences in nocturnal plant movement.' Frontiers in Plant Science 8: 1814. doi: 10.3389/fpls.2017.01814.

See also: https://www.newscientist.com/article/2167003-trees-may-have-a-heartbeat-that-is-so-slow-we-never-noticed-it/

3. Gagliano, M. *et al.* (2016) 'Learning by association in plants.' *Scientific Reports* 6: 38427. doi: 10.1038/srep38427. For a comprehensive list of fascinating research on plant behaviour and cognition, see: www.monicagagliano.com

4. Darwin, Charles (1859) *On the Origin of Species by Means of Natural Selection, or the Preservation of Favoured Races in the Struggle for Life.*

5. Janine Benyus' most celebrated work is Benyus, Janine (2002) *Biomimicry: Innovation Inspired by Nature.* 2nd edition. HarperCollins.

6. The Biomimicry Institutes defines biomimicry as *"an approach to innovation that seeks sustainable solutions to human challenges by emulating nature's time-tested patterns and strategies".* See: https://biomimicry.org

7. For a wide range of nature-inspired solutions, see: https://asknature.org

8. Many of the principles in this book are borrowed from David Holmgren and Bill Mollisons' permaculture principles. Their original work is Mollison, Bill and Holmgren, David (1978) *Permaculture One: A Perennial Agriculture for Human Settlements* Transworld

9. For more information on the Transition movement, see: https://transitionnetwork.org

10. The term 'anthropocene' was popularised by atmospheric chemist Paul J. Crutzen as a new geological epoch. Various dates for the commencement of the anthropocene have been proposed, from the start of the agricultural revolution (circa 12,000 years ago) up to 1945, the detonation of the first atomic bomb.

11. Grooten, M. and Almond, R.E.A. (Eds) (2018) *Living Planet Report – 2018: Aiming Higher.* WWF, Gland, Switzerland.

12. For sources of the information on global health contained in this chapter, please see: https://ourworldindata.org

13. Institute of Health Metrics and Evaluation (IHME) (1990–2016) *Global Burden of Disease* (GBD). Available at: http://ghdx.healthdata.org/gbd-results-tool

14. Institute of Health Metrics and Evaluation (IHME) (1990–2016) *Global Burden of Disease* (GBD). Available at: http://ghdx.healthdata.org/gbd-results-tool

15. NHS Digital (2018) *Mental Health of Children and Young People in England, 2017.*

Part 1 The benefits of being in nature

1. HM Government (2018) *A Green Future: Our 25 Year Plan to Improve the Environment.*

2. A comprehensive outline of the health benefits of being in nature are contained in the papers:
   Twohig-Bennett, C. and Jones, A, (2018) 'The health benefits of the great outdoors: A systematic review and meta-analysis of greenspace exposure and health outcomes' *Environmental Research* Vol 166, and
   Richardson, M. *et al.* (2016) 'Nature: a new paradigm for well-being and ergonomics.' *Ergonomics* 60(2), 292–305.

3. Pretty, J., Peacock, J., Sellens, M. and Griffin, M. (2005) 'The mental and physical health outcomes of green exercise.' *International Journal of Environmental Health Research* 15: 5.

4. Park, B.J., Tsunetsugu, Y., Kasetani, T., Kagawa, T., and Miyazaki, Y. (2010) 'The physiological effects of Shinrin-yoku (taking in the forest atmosphere or forest bathing): evidence from field experiments in 24 forests across Japan.' *Environmental Health and Preventive Medicine* 15(1): 18–26.

5. See: https://www.gov.uk/government/publications/five-ways-to-mental-wellbeing

6. Lumber, R., Richardson, M., and Sheffield, D. (2017) 'Beyond knowing nature: contact, emotion, compassion, meaning, and beauty are pathways to nature connection.' *PLoS ONE* 12(5): e0177186.
   https://doi.org/10.1371/journal.pone.0177186

7. Richard Louv coined the term 'Vitamin N', and has written three books on the subject: *Vitamin N: The Essential Guide to a Nature-Rich Life* (2017) Atlantic Books; *The Nature Principle: Reconnecting with Life in a Virtual Age* (2012)

Algonquin; and *Last Child in the Woods: Saving our Children from Nature-Deficit Disorder* (2010) Atlantic Books.

8. Richardson, Miles and Sheffield, David (2017) 'Three good things in nature: noticing nearby nature brings sustained increases in connection with nature.' *Psyecology* 8(1): 1–32. doi: 10.1080/21711976.2016.1267136.

9. Richardson, Miles and Sheffield, David (2017) 'Three good things in nature: noticing nearby nature brings sustained increases in connection with nature.' *Psyecology* 8(1): 1–32. doi: 10.1080/21711976.2016.1267136.

Group 1 Principles – Observation

Observe and interact

1. Chamovitz, Daniel (2017) *What a Plant Knows: A Field Guide to the Senses*. Updated and expanded edition. Macmillan, USA.

2. Csikszentmihalyi, Mihaly (2002) *Flow: The Psychology of Happiness: The Classic Work on How to Achieve Happiness*. Rider.

Be part of the natural world

1. This quote is from Lewis-Stempel, John (2018) *The Wood: The Life & Times of Cockshutt Wood*. Doubleday.

2. Louv, Richard (2010) *Last Child in the Woods: Saving our Children from Nature-Deficit Disorder*. Atlantic Books.

3. American Psychiatric Association (2013) *Diagnostic and Statistical Manual of Mental Disorders*. Fifth edition (DSM-5). American Psychiatric Publishing.

4. Bar-On, Yinon M., Phillips, Rob and Milo, Ron (2018) 'The biomass distribution on Earth.' *PNAS* 115(25): 6506–6511. https://doi.org/10.1073/pnas.1711842115

5. Wilson, Edward O. (1984) *Biophilia*. Harvard University Press, Cambridge, MA. Also Kellert, Stephen and Wilson, E.O. (1995) *The Biophilia Hypothesis*. Island Press.

6. Research and information on nature connection by Prof Miles Richardson of Derby University is discussed in his excellent blog: https://findingnature.org.uk

7. Beech, E., Rivers, M., Oldfield, S. and Smith, P.P. (2017) 'GlobalTreeSearch: the first complete global database of

tree species and country distributions.' *Journal of Sustainable Forestry* 36(5): 454-489. doi: 10.1080/10549811.2017.1310049.

8. Professor of Psychology and Environmental Studies Cindy Frantz gave the keynote address on June 20, 2018 at the Nature Connections Conference at the University of Derby in Derby, UK. Frantz's talk was titled *Connection to Nature: A Core Social Motive Approach.*

Follow nature's patterns

1. To learn more about patterns in nature I recommend the following:

Ball, Philip (2016) *Patterns in Nature. Why the World Looks the Way it Does.* University of Chicago Press.

Stewart, Ian (2017) *The Beauty of Numbers in Nature: Mathematical Patterns and Principles from the Natural World.* Ivy Press.

Learn from what's gone before

1. Adams, Max (2018) *The Wisdom of Trees: A Miscellany.* Head of Zeus.

2. Adams, Max (2018) *The Wisdom of Trees: A Miscellany.* Head of Zeus.

3. Chamovitz, Daniel (2017) *What a Plant Knows: A Field Guide to the Senses.* Updated and expanded edition. Macmillan, USA.

4. Chamovitz, Daniel (2017) *What a Plant Knows: A Field Guide to the Senses.* Updated and expanded edition. Macmillan, USA.

View the big picture then the detail

1. Lovelock, James (1979) *Gaia: A New Look at Life on Earth.* OUP, Oxford.

2. Brené Brown sets out her challenges in this regard in her brilliant book: Brown, Brené (2017) *Braving the Wilderness: The Quest for True Belonging and the Courage to Stand Alone.* Vermillion.

3. I couldn't not include a reference to *The Hitchhiker's Guide to the Galaxy* by Douglas Adams. Astute readers will also notice that the number of principles in this book equals

42, which in the *Hitchhiker's Guide* is *"The Answer to the Ultimate Question of Life, the Universe, and Everything"*, calculated by an enormous supercomputer named Deep Thought over a period of 7.5 million years (although please don't think that I am immodest enough to believe that all the answers are contained in this book).

4. For more on compassionate communication, jackal and giraffe, see the work of Dr Marshall Rosenberg, founder of the Center for Nonviolent Communication.

5. Jane Bevan, artist. See: http://www.janebevan.co.uk

Listen to your internal ecosystem

1. Adams, Max (2018) *The Wisdom of Trees: A Miscellany*. Head of Zeus.

Group 2 Principles – Purpose

Live with purpose

1. Buettner, Dan (2017) *The Blue Zones of Happiness: Lessons from the World's Happiest People*. National Geographic. See also Dan Buettner's excellent TED Talk: *How to Live To Be 100*. https://www.ted.com/talks/dan_buettner_how_to_live_to_be_100#t-1221

Don't stop growing

1. Taylor, David (2003) *The Naked Leader: The Best Selling Guide to Unlimited Success*. Bantam.

2. Carol Dweck has written a series of books, including: Dweck, Carol (2017) *Mindset: Changing The Way You Think To Fulfil Your Potential*. Updated edition. Robinson.

Learn self-regulation

1. Meadows, Donella (2013) *Leverage Points: Places to Intervene in a System*. Archived 2013-10-08 at the Wayback Machine, 1999.

2. Roszak, Theodore (2002) *Voice of the Earth: An Exploration of Ecopsychology*. Phanes Press, USA.

Catch and use energy effectively

1. Project Drawdown is the most comprehensive plan to reverse global warming. From the website www.drawdown.org: *"Project Drawdown gathers and facilitates a broad coalition of researchers, scientists, graduate students, PhDs, post-docs, policy makers, business leaders and activists to assemble and present the best available information on climate solutions in order to describe their beneficial financial, social and environmental impact over the next thirty years."* You can discover the top 80 solutions in order of impact on the website, or read the book: Hawken, Paul (2018) *Drawdown: The Most Comprehensive Plan Ever Proposed to Reverse Global Warming.* Penguin.

Find slow and small solutions

1. Thoreau, Henry David (first published 1854) *Walden, or a Life in the Woods.*
2. Csikszentmihalyi, Mihaly (2002) *Flow: The Psychology of Happiness: The Classic Work on How to Achieve Happiness.* Rider.
3. Dolan, Paul (2015) *Happiness by Design: Finding Pleasure and Purpose in Everyday Life.* Penguin.
4. For photos of the Whistlewood roundhouse, constructed from straw bales and timber, see: www.whistlewoodcommon.org. The floor is insulated with 9000 wine bottles collected by local people, and the roof is insulated with sheep's wool.

Value your uniqueness

1. In the USA: Centres for Disease Control: https://www.cdc.gov/ncbddd/adhd/medicated.html.
    In the UK: Beau-Lejdstrom, R., Douglas, I., Evans, S.J.W., *et al.* (2016) 'Latest trends in ADHD drug prescribing patterns in children in the UK: prevalence, incidence and persistence.' *BMJ Open* 6: e010508. doi: 10.1136/bmjopen-2015-010508.
2. Office for National Statistics (ONS) (Jan 2018) *Children's Engagement With the Outdoors and Sports Activities UK: 2014 to 2015.*

3. American Institutes for Research (2005) *Effects of Outdoor Education Programs for Children in California*. Palo Alto, CA.
4. Hopkins, Gerard Manley (1881) *Inversnaid.*
5. George Monbiot's book, *Feral*, advocates the rewilding of natural spaces, and recognises that almost all landscapes that we consider 'natural' are actually shaped by humans. Rewilding offers strategies to reintroduce species and allow nature to take its course, and to allow ourselves to 'rewild' our own lives. The book explores the reasons why this is so important.
    Monbiot, George (2013) *Feral: Rewilding the Land, Sea and Human Life*. Penguin.

Use your edge
1. Derek Sivers' TED Talk: *How to Start a Movement* is at: https://www.ted.com/talks/derek_sivers_how_to_start_a _movement#t-59295

Group 3 Principles – Surroundings

Create ideal conditions to thrive
1. For an explanation of the process by which this comes about, see: Wohlleben, Peter (2017) *The Hidden Life of Trees: What They Feel, How They Communicate*. William Collins, p.106. His book also references research by Anastassia Makarieva, see: Makarieva, A.M. and Gorshkov, V.G. (2007) 'Biotic pump of atmospheric moisture as driver of the hydrological cycle on land.' *Hydrology and Earth System Sciences* 11(2): 1013–33. See: www.bioticregulation.ru/ common/pdf/07e01s-hess_mg_.pdf
2. Lovelock, James (1979) *Gaia: A New Look at Life on Earth*. OUP, Oxford.

Invest in your wellbeing
1. World Health Organization at: https://www.who.int/about/mission/en/
2. Buettner, Dan (2017) *The Blue Zones of Happiness: Lessons from the World's Happiest People*. National Geographic.
3. Another of the results of the longevity studies in *Blue Zones* by Dan Buettner.

Plan for each need to be well supported
1. Looby McNamara is a pioneer in the developing field of social permaculture and wrote the influential work *People and Permaculture*, from which this and other ideas in this book were harvested.
    McNamara, Looby (2012) *People & Permaculture*. Permanent Publications.
    McNamara, Looby (2014) *7 Ways to Think Differently: Embrace Potential, Respond to Life, Discover Abundance*. Permanent Publications.
2. Boyle, Mark (2012) *The Moneyless Manifesto*. Permanent Publications.

Feed your roots
1. Wohlleben, Peter (2017) *The Hidden Life of Trees: What They Feel, How They Communicate*. William Collins, p.81.

Waste nothing, recycle everything
1. Thoreau, Henry David (first published 1854) *Walden, or a Life in the Woods*.

Group 4 Principles – Connection

Know that everything is connected
1. Peter Wohlleben describes coming across an ancient tree stump, felled approximately 400–500 years previously, that was being kept alive by the surrounding trees.
    Wohlleben, Peter (2017) *The Hidden Life of Trees: What They Feel, How They Communicate*. William Collins, pp.1–2.
2. Brown, B. (2010) *The Gifts of Imperfection: Let Go of Who You Think You're Supposed to Be and Embrace Who You Are*. Hazelden Publishing.
3. The Timber Festival takes place on the Leicestershire/Derbyshire border in the UK. See: https://timberfestival.org.uk/
4. We hosted people under the WWOOF scheme (Worldwide Opportunities on Organic Farms). See: http://wwoof.net/

Value diversity

1. There are widely diverging estimates on the number of species. Wikipedia presents the evidence at: https://en.wikipedia.org/wiki/Biodiversity
2. Beech, E., Rivers, M., Oldfield, S. and Smith, P.P. (2017) 'GlobalTreeSearch: the first complete global database of tree species and country distributions.' *Journal of Sustainable Forestry* 36(5): 454-489. doi: 10.1080/10549811.2017.1310049.
3. British Member of Parliament, Helen Joanne Cox (Jo Cox) was murdered in June 2016 by Thomas Mair, who held far-right views. Her maiden speech in the House of Commons on 3 June 2015 included the following words: "*...we are far more united and have far more in common than that which divides us.*" Since her death, the Jo Cox Foundation has continued working on the causes she was passionate about, and have organised '*Great get-together*' events around the UK, bringing communities together to celebrate kindness, respect and all they have in common. See: http://www.greatgettogether.org/

Cultivate co-operative relationships

1. Dawkins, R. (1978) *The Selfish Gene.* OUP.
2. Dawkins, R. (2017) *The Ancestor's Tale: A Pilgrimage to the Dawn of Life.* W&N.
3. Cancer Research UK
   https://www.cancerresearchuk.org/health-professional/cancer-statistics/risk/lifetime-risk
   Lifetime risk estimates calculated by the Statistical Information Team at Cancer Research UK. Based on Office for National Statistics (ONS) *2016-Based Life Expectancies and Population Projections.* Accessed December 2017, and Smittenaar, C.R., Petersen, K.A., Stewart, K. and Moitt, N. (2016) 'Cancer incidence and mortality projections in the UK until 2035.' *British Journal of Cancer.*
   Ahmad, A.S., Ormiston-Smith, N. and Sasieni, P.D. (2015) 'Trends in the lifetime risk of developing cancer in Great Britain: comparison of risk for those born in 1930 to 1960.' *British Journal of Cancer.* bjc.2014:606.

4. A fascinating book about super-organisms found in nature and their relevance to business and social structures is: Wooley-Barker, Tamsin (2017) *Teeming: How Superorganisms Work Together to Build Infinite Wealth on a Finite Planet (and your company can too)*. White Cloud Press.

Integrate don't segregate

1. Roszak, Theodore (2002) *Voice of the Earth: An Exploration of Ecopsychology*. Phanes Press, USA.
2. Apples and Honey Nightingale House, London, UK
3. Humanitas Residential and Care Centre, Deventer, Netherlands.
4. Holt-Lunstad, J., Smith, T.B., Baker, M., Harris, T. and Stephenson, D. (2015) 'Loneliness and social isolation as risk factors for mortality: a meta-analytic review.' *Perspectives on Psychological Science* 10(2): 227. doi: 10.1177/1745691614568352.
5. Flannery, Tim in Wohlleben, Peter (2017) *The Hidden Life of Trees: What They Feel, How They Communicate*. William Collins, p.viii.
6. www.lilac.coop

Pick your battles

1. Rachel Carson, marine biologist and conservationist, author of *Silent Spring* (1962), is widely regarded as an early pioneer of the environmental movement. Her work led to the creation of the US Environmental Protection Agency. Carson, Rachel (1962) *Silent Spring*. Houghton Mifflin Company.

Share the abundance

1. Tudge, Colin (2006) *The Secret Life of Trees: How They Live and Why They Matter*. Penguin Press Science, p.3.
2. Joanna Macy is an environmental scholar. Her works are considered as part of the Deep Ecology movement and include: Macy, Joanna and Young Brown, Molly (1998) *Coming Back to Life: Practices to Reconnect Our Lives, Our World*. New Society Publishers; and Macy, Joanna and Johnstone, Chris (2012) *Active Hope: How To Face The Mess We're In Without Going Crazy*. New World Library.

3. Charities Aid Foundation (2015) *UK Giving 2014* at https://www.cafonline.org/docs/default-source/about-us-publications/caf-ukgiving2014.pdf?sfvrsn=104dfb40_4

4. The Equality Trust (2017) *Pay Tracker Comparing Chief Executive Officer Pay in the FTSE 100 with Average Pay and Low Pay in the UK.* https://www.equalitytrust.org.uk/sites/default/files/resou rce/attachments/Pay%20Tracker%20%20-%20web_0.pdf

5. The Equality Trust https://www.equalitytrust.org.uk/trust-participation-attitudes-and-happiness

Group 5 Principles – Resilience

Know that life is a struggle

1. This amazing fact came from the BBC TV series *Life, (Plants)* (2009), narrated by Sir David Attenborough.

Creatively respond to change

1. A discussion of this research is contained in Csikszentmihalyi, Mihaly (2002) *Flow: The Psychology of Happiness: The Classic Work on How to Achieve Happiness.* Rider, Chapter 9.

2. If you have a private pension, switching to an ethical pension is a really 'easy win' on ethical/environmental grounds. You may get to specify which ethical considerations are more important to you. There are often no, or marginal, differences in yield. If you have a company pension, petition the pension provider to divest of fossil fuels, tobacco and arms, as many already have. On financial grounds, you might also want to consider whether having your money invested in fossil fuels is a good idea, given the big switch to renewables.

3. Harari, Yuval Noah (2015) *Sapiens: A Brief History of Humankind.* Vintage.

4. The term 'positive disintegration' is thanks to Joanna Macy. See Macy, Joanna and Young Brown, Molly (1998) *Coming Back to Life: Practices to Reconnect Our Lives, Our World.* New Society Publishers.

5. Solutions thinking is one of the 'ways of thinking differently' discussed in Looby McNamara's book: McNamara, Looby (2014) *7 Ways to Think Differently: Embrace Potential, Respond to Life, Discover Abundance.* Permanent Publications.

6. Edward de Bono has written many books on different ways of thinking, including de Bono, Edward (1967) *The Use of Lateral Thinking.* Penguin.

In the *Think like a Tree* courses we also use the tool, *Six Thinking Hats* – de Bono, Edward (Latest edition 2016) *Six Thinking Hats.* Penguin.

7. Elephant bones dating from this period are on display at Derby Museum, UK.

Seek and offer support

1. The American Psychological Association's website is a great source of information and research on resilience. https://www.apa.org/helpcenter/road-resilience.aspx

2. Dr Martin Seligman is the founder of Positive Psychology and has written several books, including: Seligman, Martin (2017) *Authentic Happiness: Using the New Positive Psychology to Realise your Potential for Lasting Fulfilment.* Nicholas Brealey Publishing.

3. A discussion of Dunbar's number, with references, is contained in the Wikipedia entry: https://en.wikipedia.org/wiki/Dunbar%27s_number#cite _note-dunbar92–1

Learn to heal yourself

1. Jones, J.D.G and Dangl, J.L. (2006) 'The plant immune system.' *Nature* 444: 323–329.

2. Puttonen, Eetu *et al.* (2016) 'Quantification of overnight movement of birch (*Betula pendula*) branches and foliage with short interval terrestrial laser scanning.' *Frontiers in Plant Science.*

3. Ulrich, R.S. (1983) 'Aesthetic and affective response to natural environment.' *Human Behavior and Environment: Advances in Theory & Research* 6: 85–125.

4. Duckworth, A.L., Peterson, C., Matthews, M.D. and Kelly, D.R. (2007) 'Grit: perseverance and passion for long-term

Think like a Tree

goals.' *Journal of Personality and Social Psychology* 92(6): 1087–1101.

Tune into natural cycles

1. You can see a short video of the changes at Yellowstone National Park (video created by Sustainable Human and narrated by George Monbiot) at:
https://www.youtube.com/watch?v=ysa5OBhXz-Q
Also an explanation of the changes by Yellowstone National Park at:
https://www.yellowstonepark.com/things-to-do/wolf-reintroduction-changes-ecosystem

Group 6 Principles – Future

Create conditions conducive to life

1. For information on attachment styles, see Mikulincer, M. and Shaver, R. (2001) 'Attachment theory and intergroup bias: evidence that priming the secure base schema attenuates negative reactions to out-groups.' *Journal of Personality and Social Psychology* 81: 97–115.

2. Resolution 65/309 adopted by the UN General Assembly on 19 July 2011: 'Happiness: towards a holistic approach to development' states: *"Conscious that the pursuit of happiness is a fundamental human goal…Recognising that the gross domestic product indicator by nature was not designed and does not adequately reflect the happiness and well-being of people in a country. Invites Member States to pursue the elaboration of additional measures that better capture the importance of the pursuit of happiness and well-being in development with a view to guiding their public policies".* For the full text of the resolution, see: http://www.un.org/en/ga/search/view_doc.asp?symbol=A/RES/65/309

3. UK national wellbeing is measured by the Office for National Statistics. The most recent report is from 2018. *Personal Well-being in the UK: July 2017 to June 2018. Estimates of Life Satisfaction, Feeling That the Things Done in Life are Worthwhile, Happiness and Anxiety at the UK and Country Level.* Available at:

246

https://www.ons.gov.uk/peoplepopulationandcommunity/wellbeing/bulletins/measuringnationalwellbeing/july2017tojune2018

4. The King of Bhutan coined the phrase *Gross National Happiness* in 1972. For information about Bhutan's happiness measures, see: *The Constitution of Bhutan* at http://www.nationalcouncil.bt/assets/uploads/files/Constitution%20%20of%20Bhutan%20English.pdf

5. There is a great variety of different methods for participation, and many are set out by the organisation *Involve* at: https://www.involve.org.uk/resources/methods

Replicate and build on strategies that work
1. UNCTAD (2013) *Trade and Environmental Review: Wake Up Before It's Too Late.* United Nations Conference on Trade and Development. See also Rodale Institute (2014) *Regenerative Organic Agriculture and Climate Change.*

2. Halweil, Brian (2006) 'Can organic agriculture feed us all?' *World Watch Magazine* 19(3).

3. https://www.yeovalley.co.uk/the-farm

4. https://www.charlesdowding.co.uk/

5. Akinnifesi, F.K., Makumba, W. and Kwesiga, F.R. (2006) 'Sustainable maize production using gliricidia/maize intercropping in southern Malawi.' *Experimental Agriculture* 42: 441–457. doi:10.1017/S0014479706003814. Archived from the original pdf on 2014-07-14.

6. https://www.savory.global/. See also: https://www.ted.com/talks/allan_savory_how_to_green_the_world_s_deserts_and_reverse_climate_change

7. https://www.permaculture.co.uk/videos/watch-bbcs-visit-stunning-forest-garden

8. https://communitysupportedagriculture.org.uk

9. https://www.fordhallfarm.com/

10. http://www.citycommonscsa.com/

11. http://wwoof.net/

12. Transition Network: https://transitionnetwork.org/
In the USA, see: http://transitionus.org/our-story. Also the excellent books by Transition founder Rob Hopkins including: Hopkins, Rob (2013) *The Power of Just Doing Stuff: How Local Action Can Change the world.* Green Books; and

Hopkins, Rob (2011) *The Transition Companion: Making Your Community More Resilient in Uncertain Times*. Transition Books.

13. https://www.transitiontowntotnes.org/
14. https://12020.org/
15. https://biomimicry.org/
16. https://www.stocorp.com/
17. https://www.columbiaforestproducts.com
18. http://www.bullittcenter.org/
19. http://www.mickpearce.com/Eastgate.html
20. https://www.stefanoboeriarchitetti.net/en/
21. http://www.calera.com
22. http://www.solarbotanic.com/
23. https://asknature.org/idea/concentrated-solar-plant/#.XGaF6PZ2vIU
24. http://www.atder-bl.org/
25. In the USA, see: New Economy Coalition (NEC) https://neweconomy.net/
In the UK, see New Economics Foundation https://neweconomics.org/
26. Jackson's second edition is: Jackson, Tim (revised edition 2016) *Prosperity Without Growth: Foundations for the Economy of Tomorrow*. Routledge.
27. For a discussion on the role of growth in the economies of the future see Wahl, Daniel Christian (2016) *Designing Regenerative Cultures*. Triarchy Press. This book is a valuable source of information on a wide-range of issues and regenerative solutions on the subjects of culture, agriculture, economics, business and society.
28. http://www.ethicalmarkets.com/category/green-transition-scoreboard/
29. https://www.buurtzorg.com
30. For a discussion of Sun Hydraulics corporate systems, see Woolley-Brown, Tamsin (2017) *Teeming*. White Cloud Press.
31. A discussion of FAVI is also in Woolley-Brown, Tamsin (2017) *Teeming*. White Cloud Press.
32. Hawkin, Paul (2018) *Drawdown: The Most Comprehensive Plan Ever Proposed to Reverse Global Warming*. Penguin. See also: https://www.drawdown.org

Be a good ancestor

1. One source of information is: Ethical Consumer https://www.ethicalconsumer.org/
   The Co-operative Bank's ethical policy is a good resource for researching the issues that the UK's bank's customers raise as areas of concern (or those they wish to support). https://www.co-operativebank.co.uk/assets/pdf/bank/aboutus/ethicalpolicy/ethical-policy.pdf

2. One way of pushing governments and corporations to act is by supporting change via the law, such as those pioneered by Client Earth, an organisation of lawyers using the law to bring governments to account. See: https://www.clientearth.org/

3. 2005 research showed that some consumers actively avoid knowing about the ethical aspects of their purchases. Ehrich, Kristine R. and Irwin, Julie R. (2005) 'Willful ignorance in the request for product attribute information.' *Journal of Marketing Research* 42(3): 266–277. The report states: *"Negative emotions, especially the avoidance of anger, appear to drive this willful ignorance"*.

Know that your actions can change the world

1. A wide variety of resources, books and audiobooks are on Brené Brown's website. See: https://brenebrown.com. Her TED Talks on belonging are at https://www.ted.com

2. Rifkin, Jeremy (2013) *The Empathic Civilization: The Race to Global Consciousness in a World in Crisis.* Tarcher.

3. Brown, Brené (2017) *Braving the Wilderness: The Quest for True Belonging and the Courage to Stand Alone.* Vermillion.

Love life!

1. Eisenstein, Charles (2018) *Climate: A New Story.* North Atlantic Books.

Made in the USA
Columbia, SC
01 August 2020